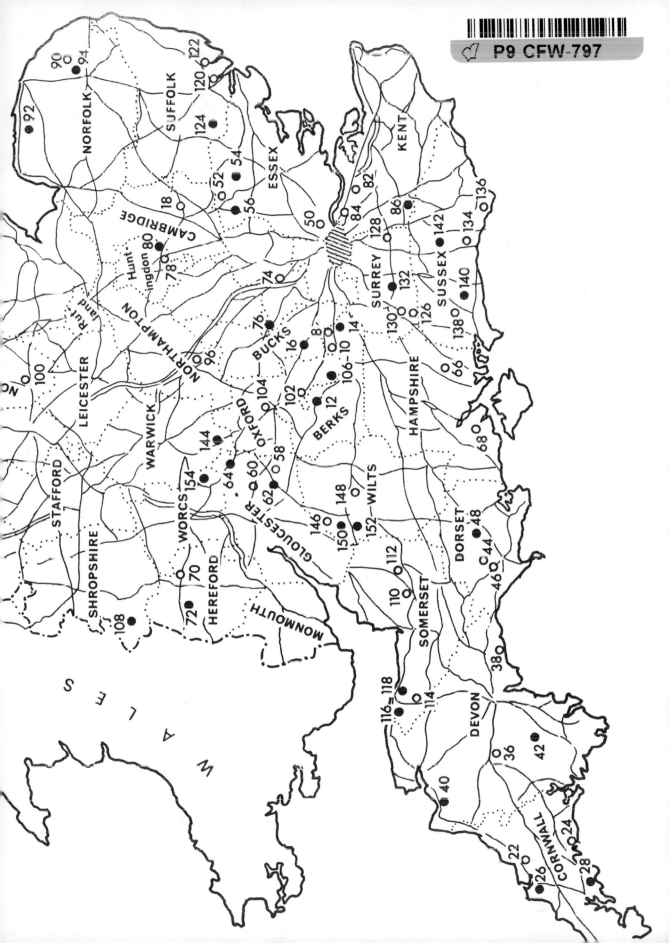

INNS AND VILLAGES OF ENGLAND

INNS AND VILLAGES OF ENGLAND

by

GARRY HOGG

ARCO PUBLISHING COMPANY, INC.
NEW YORK

In travelling thro' England, a luxuriance of objects presents it self to our view: Where ever we come, and which way so ever we look, we see something new, something significant, something well worth the traveller's stay.

Daniel Defoe

Published in the United States by
Arco Publishing Company, Inc.
219 Park Avenue South, New York, N.Y. 10003
Second Printing, 1968
© George Newnes Ltd. 1966
Library of Congress Card Number: 66-21264
Arco Catalog Number: 1489

MADE AND PRINTED IN THE REPUBLIC OF IRELAND
BY HELY THOM LIMITED, DUBLIN

AUTHOR'S FOREWORD

The problem of containing a quart within a pint pot could hardly be better demonstrated than in this attempt to portray, in a hundred-and-fifty-odd pages, the beauty, interest and variety of the innumerable villages and rural inns to be found in England. Justice could scarcely be done to them in a volume six times the size.

It really is remarkable that in so highly urbanised and industrialised a country as England there should still exist so many unspoiled villages. What is more, they are often to be found not only in remote and inaccessible corners but almost within sight and sound of the great urban centres. Unhappily, their days are numbered. Yet even in this second half of a twentieth century that is fast turning us all into mechanised animals in mechanised lairs, villages of character are to be found by the thousand: an *embarras de richesses* indeed when it comes to making a fair and representative selection from among them.

The rural inns, too, exist in their thousands. Every village, no matter how small, has one at least; it may have several. And happily for the tourist they are also to be found strung out along the roadside. They punctuate the greater and lesser roads (though not, of course, the new motorways), spaced out between town and town, village and village. Some, of course, are threatened by road-widening schemes; the more fortunate nestle in backwaters, along the twisting lanes not yet scheduled for widening; soon, may be, to be bypassed. The restless motorist, intent upon maintaining high averages, will probably miss them altogether—to his certain loss.

Some of these inns, it is true, have fallen prey to the speculator, have been given most unsuitable face-lifts, and so have lost for ever their true and traditional character. This book naturally ignores these. But happily there are many hundreds left that have been spared this indignity. With very few exceptions, having rather special claims for inclusion—Nottingham's *Trip to Jerusalem* is one such; another is *The Fighting Cocks* at St. Albans—the inns selected are the truly rural ones: hostelries, that is to say, which stand isolated by the roadside or, at most, are an integral element of some village or small market township. They are unlikely to rate stars in the motoring associations' various handbooks.

Every one of them, however, is known to me personally. I discovered many of them in those halcyon days, forty-odd years ago, when there was room for a cyclist fresh from the classroom to start half a lifetime's exploration of the countryside. Beneath many of their homely roofs I ate and slept, when it was possible to obtain 'Bed and Breakfast' for little more than one pays today for a packet of twenty cigarettes. I have been back to many of them time and again since those far-off days, delighted when I have found that they have not fundamentally changed in appearance and atmosphere—even if their charges have inevitably soared.

At most of the inns you can obtain a meal—often a very good one indeed; or at any rate an excellent snack-at-the-bar. At many of them you can obtain overnight accommodation: simple, clean, satisfying. And at all of them, of course, you can obtain liquid refreshment. At all of them, too, I can assure you, you will find much that is of interest other than food and drink and a bed. Even the remotest will amply repay the time and the occasional detailed map reading involved in tracking them down.

As for the villages: suggestions came from many quarters, none of them to be ignored. It is a measure of their great number that there was so little overlapping between one list and another.

As with the inns, the only thing to do was to go out and renew acquaintance with them for myself. This involved covering some eight thousand miles of roads. Mostly these were the lesser roads, the byways and lanes, within a triangle having for its points the Cheviot Hills, Thanet, and Land's End.

No other country offers anything comparable with the variety of the English village. Each village has its individual claim for inclusion. Had I restricted myself to one region alone—the Cotswolds, for example, or Kent and Sussex, or the Ridings of Yorkshire, or the Lake District—I should have found it easy enough to reach the tally prescribed, and also to illustrate this infinite variety. But I wished, so far as the villages were concerned, to offer an overall picture of the English village as it survives—often in spite of the shocking hazards of urban and industrial encroachment—today. My aim, also, was to achieve a balance between the purely picturesque, the essentially photogenic, on the one hand; on the other, to give what might be called the 'story' behind each village, each inn.

Villages existed long before towns and cities. With their nucleus of church, inn, school, and occasional 'Great House' on the outskirts, the domain of the local squire and his family for generations past, may be centuries, they possess a unity, an integrity, not to be found amongst the greater conurbations. I know every one of these villages well. To many of them I have returned again and again over the years, temporarily forsaking the main route of some necessary journey for the sheer pleasure of renewing acquaintance with some place visited at intervals over a period of forty years and more.

I returned from my quest with subjects running into several hundreds, and photographs to match. Only then did the labour begin. To reduce hundreds to scores, and scores to a total of seventy-odd, involved labour which, it is hardly an exaggeration to say, was fraught with anguish. So many deserving candidates clamoured to be let in; for so many of them there, quite literally, was no room. So many choices were invidious. And already I hear the advance-guard of protest among lovers of our countryside: Where are (for example) Chilham and Tissington, Ashprington and Bicknoller, Linton-in-Craven, Grange-in-Borrodale and Hutton-le-Hole? And where, too, The Shaven Crown, the Falkland Arms, The Old Albion and Cowper's Oak, The Greyhound at Corfe and Journey's End at Ringmore, Devon? Alas, where indeed?

For the most part I have selected villages whose inns are not mentioned, and inns whose containing villages are not featured. This was deliberate guile: the enterprising tourist will thus happen upon the one when specifically in search of the other, and thus more often than not obtain 'two for the price of one'.

The months spent in search of material were among the most rewarding I have spent in years. The weeks spent in reducing the mass of material to manageable proportions, inevitably dictated by the economics of publishing, were less happy. Inadequately representative as this selection must necessarily be, it may encourage you to go out in search of what is here portrayed in picture and text and discover for yourselves—and the more unexpectedly the better—the inexhaustible riches that await you, just round the next corner, and the next one after that. But: the face of England is changing all the time; so, do not put off your own quest too long.

G.H.

GROOMBRIDGE, SUSSEX.

The inns and villages described and illustrated in the following pages have been arranged, for easy reference, in alphabetical order of counties—the inns first and then the villages.

BOULTER'S INN, Boulter's Lock, Berkshire (*Alongside A4094, two miles from Maidenhead*).

For a lover of rivers, boats, fishing, no inn could be better placed. It stands on a small island between the Thames lock and the main stream flowing beneath its many balconied windows. From these you look out across the water and the passing dinghies, yachts and motor-launches to a backcloth of terraced trees rising from the bank side beyond. It is an idyllic scene of which you will never grow tired.

The inn makes no claim to distinction of age. Little more than half a century ago the island contained a flour mill; corn and wheat were ground here for generations by the Fullers, who combined milling with brewing; the Thames water operated enormous millstones weighing a ton and more apiece. But the lease expired, the mill was abandoned, and the millers' house was enlarged and altered to answer the purpose of an inn. It was named, like the adjacent lock, 'Boulters', after the old word for a miller.

Brightly painted verandahs, terraces reaching down to water level so that you may step off them into your boat, or on to them from it, balconies beneath overhanging gables, a house embowered in trees that rise above its roof: these amenities, and, above all, the smoothly-sliding Thames at your feet, beneath your windows, sprinkled with craft large and small, offer so much that it would be a grasping individual who demanded more. There is always something going on, and the atmosphere is always one of cheerfulness, to match the colour and movement of the water flowing by. If you wish to explore, however, this is a good base from which to range the river banks: a mile or two in one direction and you are within hail of Medmenham Abbey and the ghosts of the notorious 'Hell-Fire Club', of Bisham Abbey and the restless ghost of Lady Hoby. And in the opposite direction you will come to Runnymede and the site of the signing of Magna Carta. History comes alive on this stretch of the river.

8

THE BULL, Sonning, Berkshire (*On B748, five miles east of Reading*).

Leaving the river bank, you pass through the churchyard of the flint-and-stone Church of St Andrew, parts of which date back to Norman times, and emerge direct into the courtyard formed by the L-shaped, fifteenth-century inn and the churchyard wall, overshadowed pleasantly by well-grown trees. Sacred and secular, as so often up and down the country, rub elbows here, their age separated only by a century or two. Look upwards. Chimneys cluster above the roof; dormer windows thrust through the mellow tiles, their gables rising like surprised eyebrows above the close-set, discreet small panes; clematis weaves its leisurely way among them, to break the whiteness of the plasterwork between the beams.

Within, low, heavily-beamed ceilings remind you that men were smaller five centuries ago than they are today. Until recently these fine beams were barely suspected beneath thick plaster; its removal revealed them, the carpenters' adze-marks shining in the flames of the hearth which, too, was revealed when an ugly superimposed iron fireplace was thrown out. On either side of it are recesses where, formerly, ale was mulled. So, the inn today closely resembles what its habituees knew long ago.

Why is it called *The Bull*? Some four centuries ago the first Queen Elizabeth did a deal in Royal Properties with the Bishop of Salisbury. She then appointed Sir Henri Nevill Steward-in-Chief to her newly acquired property. The knight's coat-of-arms bore the device of a bull, and this was transferred to the inn. On the edge of a sleepy village, it is a quieter place today than it was four hundred years ago when the Bishop, with a great retinue for his dignity and protection, slept here on his way to the Queen's Court, his men and beasts occupying the outbuildings.

BLEWBURY, Berkshire (*On A417, nine miles east of Wantage*).

Lying in a hollow of the Berkshire Downs, this enchanting village has successfully preserved its integrity and air of seclusion despite the proximity of an important east-west main road and the activities of the race-horse owners whose strings of horses are continually silhouetted on the smooth skylines to the south. The true 'magic' of the village lies to the north. Here you will become lost in a network of little lanes bordered by hedges behind which there nestle thatched and half-timbered cottages each more lovely than the last, with its mellow brick, its cream or whitewash, its lead-paned windows half-hidden beneath brows of thatch, its old-world garden filled with fruit trees that seem everlastingly covered with blossom or generously spilling apples and pears.

Above all, the magic lies in the curious network of small twisting streamlets that duck beneath the weeping-willows, glint in the dappled shade and emerge just now and then into full view when they are spanned by a footbridge carrying a narrow path that links cottage with cottage, lane with lane. Follow almost any one of these, and you will find yourself between high cob walls unexpectedly topped with thatch— a feature practically unique to Blewbury. They have a protective, endearing quality. It is small wonder that artists and writers have haunted this place, these paths and miniature waterways, for generations past. Here, not surprisingly, Kenneth Grahame found the inspiration for his *Wind in the Willows*; here he found the true setting for the immortal story of Badger, Ratty, Mole, and Toad of Toad Hall. And fifteen centuries ago an Irish saint, Birinus, strode here to convert the people to his faith. He took a chalk track now known as Rubble-pit Lane. The villagers will show you where his footsteps lay, for chalk-born wild flowers grow in them to this day.

BRAY, Berkshire (*Off A308, one mile south of Maidenhead*).

The road to the river curves through this small village, skirting the famous Hinds Head hostelry and the seventeenth-century almshouses still known as *Jesus Hospital*. A narrow alley, Church Lane, leads you past a row of ancient, white-painted cottages to the remarkable lych-gate known as the Gate House, almost unique of its kind. The passage beneath it is twenty feet long by eight feet wide and little over six feet high. It has carried on its enormous timbers, one of which bears the date 1448, a solid brick and timber cottage that has been lived in for five centuries and is lived in still. On your right hand, hidden in shadow, is a small door leading to a steep, narrow staircase lit oddly by a window set in an open balustrade. Beyond, the original splendid roof-truss may be seen: evidence of the craftsmanship and quality of timber that went into the construction.

It is the gateway into the churchyard of the thirteenth-century Church of St Michael, largely built of flint and the hard chalk locally known as 'clunch' that is so beautifully veined. Here, under Henry VIII, Elizabeth I and Mary, the famous (or notorious) 'Vicar of Bray' held office, becoming in turn Papist, Protestant, and Papist once more, having watched martyrs burned at the stake at Windsor, not far away. Challenged as a turncoat, he retorted: 'I Keep to my Principle—to Live and Die Vicar of Bray'. In so pleasant a spot, with a church so memorable and the Thames so near, he can hardly be blamed for the 'tender temper which found the martyrs' fire too hot'. He occupied the gatehouse you have just left; his congregation passed beneath his feet to the church. They still pass that way, though he is long dead. It is symbolic: why should anything change in this quiet, historic spot?

WEST WYCOMBE, Buckinghamshire (*On A40, three miles west of High Wycombe*).

Happily, though it lies astride a busy main road, it is National Trust property, and so may hope to be preserved against the ravages of modernisation. Its powerful atmosphere of serenity will slow you down; which is as well, for otherwise you might pass through without having savoured any of its manifold treasures.

Leave the main road and, on foot, explore the narrow lanes that rise steeply on the north side; in particular, Church Lane. It is here that the richest treasures await you. The entrance is beneath the square archway of the ancient Church Loft. Pause before passing through. It is some four hundred years old: a two-storeyed building of brick panels in timber, projecting over the pavement almost to the road. Part of a medieval monastic establishment, it was built to house pilgrims passing between London and the West. One of its massive vertical timbers is supported by an enormous unhewn stone block. Its upper face has a concave recess, worn smooth as glass by the knees of hundreds of thousands of pious travellers who have lingered to worship at this medieval wayside shrine, their eyes raised to a cross rudely inscribed in the beam above their heads.

Pass under the archway. A massive barred door on your left marks the ancient lock-up. In front of you, a lane slopes steeply upwards to the Church of St Lawrence overlooking the village. On either side of you are gracious Georgian buildings. Also, the sixteenth-century Old Vicarage, once part of this monastic establishment. Here, as elsewhere, tradition lies all about you. Memories of Sir Francis Dashwood and the notorious Hell-Fire Club are inherent in houses large and small, sacred and secular. Perhaps no other village hides so much that is strange behind so innocent a face!

THE PLOUGH, Fen Ditton, Cambridgeshire (*Off A45, three miles east of Cambridge*).

Here is an inn most beautifully sited. It stands beside the Cam, separated from the river only by a spacious lawn that slopes gently down towards the bank. Here a hand-operated ferry links the inn with the meadows on the further side. You cross the river with circumspection, for in term time it is busy with oarsmen being coached from the towpath beneath the weeping-willows; later they will pass by in Fours and Eights, training for the inter-college 'Lents' and 'Mays', for Henley, for the varsity Boat Race. The year-round denizens of the Cam are the swans that cruise idly here, indifferent alike to punt, passing craft, the coaches' megaphone-amplified voices, the rattle and sweep of the oars.

The bay windows of the inn look out across the lawn in spring and summer alive with undergraduettes and their blazer-clad escorts, alighting from punts, canoes and rowing-boats to relax in sun or shade, idling away the endless afternoons of term. What better way to pass an hour or two, or more, than on this same greensward, within sight of the river, the boats, the swans? The busy university is but a mile or two distant across the meadows, yet out of earshot; here at Fen Ditton you will be oblivious of it, as though in a twentieth-century Garden of Eden. Impossible to contemplate any sort of work, here! And as though to emphasize that very point, you will observe that the sign *The Plough* represents not a plough team in the field, or even a plough laid up for the summer months; rather, it is the constellation known to all by that name. It is a myriad light-years away from us in time, yet probably the most familiar celestial object after the sun and the moon; it nicely stresses the remoteness of this hamlet, and its homely inn, from the rest of the world.

PRESTBURY, Cheshire (*On A538, three miles north of Macclesfield*).

It is not easy to believe, as you stand beneath the trees overhanging the main street of this Cheshire village, that you are barely ten straight miles from Manchester. For here all is peace. Little traffic passes through; the shops are quiet; the very air is still. All about you is the russet sandstone of the region: neither red nor brown, with hints of grey and grey-green, it seems to vary with the changes of light and shadow falling upon it.

On both sides of you are buildings of this stone, roofed with Kerridge slabs. Interspersed among them are fine examples of Cheshire half-timbering: jet-black oak beams, vertical, horizontal, diagonal, interlocked, with brilliant snow-white plaster in-filling. They stand out boldly among the mellower stone, with their small, close-set, diamond-paned lattice windows, withdrawn, discreet. The church, among the trees, has relics of its twelfth-century foundation, notably a doorway to the original chapel. Beyond it, the street twists and drops to a stone bridge that carries it over the Bollin, to climb again. Southwards, the village is limited by the galaxy of ornamental chimneys soaring above the Hall. Midway along the street, set back against the wall beneath the trees, stands a pair of ancient stocks, generously designed to accommodate three miscreants in a row. Nearly opposite stands the most striking building of all: the tall, narrow, massively timbered 'Priest's House'—now a bank.

A strong corporate spirit pervades this village. Not so long ago, Authority planned to drive a wide main road clean through it, to link two industrial centres; Prestbury fought back—and for once Authority submitted to intelligent pressure. As a result, you see this serene village but little changed down the centuries.

JAMAICA INN, Bolventor, Cornwall (*On A30, eight miles north-east of Bodmin*).

It stands near the highest road summit on bleak Bodmin Moor, one of the most notorious of all coaching inns. Notorious rather than merely famous, because though its great cobbled courtyard is scored deep by the iron-shod wheels of the coaches that halted here en route for Truro and Falmouth, this unprepossessing moorland inn was also the rendezvous of smugglers carrying contraband from the Cornish coves to this hiding-place and distribution centre. Within these massive walls they could feel safe.

Let the heavy door slam to behind you. It is unlikely that anywhere else, even in Cornwall, you will sense a more powerful atmosphere. It pervades the single great room, with its enormous granite fireplace, hewn out of rock, surely, not built by masons; its flagged floor worn smooth by generations of heavy feet; its tree-trunk-like oak pillars and equally massive transverse joists; its mementoes and relics—dark-lanterns, swords, horse-pistols, smugglers' brandy-kegs, Excise Men's powder-flasks. Shadows that are almost palpable fill the corners, where a man might hide within yards of his fellows, and not be seen, drinking in Mary's or Joss's Bar.

Familiar names, somehow? Of course; for this was the inspiration of Daphne du Maurier's novel, *Jamaica Inn*. The names of her characters appear in Gothic script, on narrow doors opening off the winding corridor at the head of the steep stairs; you eat, drink, perhaps sleep, in rooms bearing these immortal names. You can touch the beam with the iron hook in it from which Mary Yellan believed she saw a dangling corpse. From your window you look across the courtyard at the stage-coach moored at the road side; brooding over it, with a fierce snarl on his lips, is Joss Merlin himself, black patch over his eye, tricorne on his head, a signboard embodiment of evil.

OLD FERRY INN, Bodinnick, Cornwall (*On the estuary, immediately opposite Fowey*).

So steep is the hill at whose foot it stands, so close-set the two sides of the cutting, that you have a powerful impression that this inn has been literally hewn out of the solid rock immediately behind it. It stands a few yards above the ferry from which it takes its name, linking the east bank of the river with the picturesque township on the west. From its windows you look out across the estuary, at the beetle-like ferry-boat continuously plying between bank and bank; there is ever-lastingly something to watch, here; indeed, having once dropped your anchor at this inn you may well find it almost impossible to tear yourself away.

Steps lead to a little porch, black-painted like the windows and doors in vivid contrast to the dazzling whiter-than-white of the façade; the swinging, gold-lettered sign carries a model ship in full sail. Having entered, your impression of this having been rock hewn is at once confirmed. At every turn, natural rock is in evidence: the stairway is of rock, with slate-stone landing; ferns grow in a grotto of living rock with a glint of cool water slipping down among them. Through a gap just beyond the grotto a stone path leads you steeply upwards to an imaginatively conceived terrace, a glass-enclosed observation-chamber where you can sit by the hour and contemplate the estuary and the boats large and small that glide over it.

When you are summoned to your meal it will be by a peremptory clang on a ship's bell. It was salvaged from an oil-tanker sunk in 1941. Now it is slung from its mountings alongside the stairway, well burnished bell-metal inscribed with its name: *Erodono*. It is fitting that it should have been given a new lease of useful life here in a house having such close associations with water and ships moving upon it.

24

LITTLE PETHERICK, Cornwall (*On A389, two miles south of Padstow*).

Its original name—a heavyweight of a name for so diminutive a hamlet—is St Petroc Minor of Nansfounteyn. It commemorates the saint who, some time in the sixth century, came by coracle from Ireland, accompanied by two men, Croidan and Medan, and a boy named Dagan, who was to become a bishop, and set to work to convert the Cornish people. They formed a brotherhood of monks and became outstanding for the asceticism of their ways. Not the harshest of their practices was the reciting of their psalters by the hour while standing up to their necks in the ice-cold water of the streams that flowed, and still flow, through the clefts of the local granite.

A narrow road dips steeply to an ancient stone bridge in the heart of the village and then climbs as steeply away from it. This was the original pack-horse track that linked the port of Padstow with Wadebridge and the county town of Bodmin fifteen miles distant on the moor. It is hardly an exaggeration to say that it carries less traffic today than it did centuries ago. Part way up the hill, almost completely engulfed by trees, stands the little fourteenth-century Church of St Petroc. Against its cold grey stone the brilliant sky-blue-and-gold of the clock face stands out at once boldly and picturesquely. Two of its bells are medieval. And within the church a slab of slate from the famous Delabole quarries twenty miles away records the names of the rectors of St Petroc dating back to 1264.

This is a very silent village, even for Cornwall. The water can hardly be heard flowing beneath the bridge; the corn mill beside it no longer operates; the steep hill on either side is so thick-set with trees that the village is screened from the world beyond. It could hardly have been more quiet when St Petroc first entered it.

PORTLOE, Cornwall (*Two miles east of A3078, between St Mawes and St Austell*).

This delectable Cornish fishing village hides in a small creek of its own midway along the bold curve of Veryan Bay, a few miles from the peninsula of Saint-Anthony-in-Roseland. To reach it, you descend a lane that narrows and steepens with every hundred yards, between tall, hedge-topped banks—to emerge unexpectedly in the true heart of Portloe, the diminutive but ever busy slipway.

Village, even hamlet, seems too grandiose a term. For there is little more than an eyebrow of cottages, stone and slate built, curving round the edge of the creek and rising to the headland beyond, the church and the castle of St Michael Caerhays. Beneath them, on the other side of the road that skirts their front doors, the springy, heather-clad turf drops steeply to the rocks and deep blue water below, intersected by rough stone steps and tracks that only a goat or a nimble child can negotiate. Parents can look almost vertically down on their offspring at play on the slopes, diving from the rocks into the clear water; or on the slipway which is, of course, the focal point of the community's interests.

Here are a few small boats; here, in abundance, barrels of tar, tins of paint, coils of rope, cork floats and witch-balls, nets, lobster-pots, rusting anchors, discarded oars, tattered sail-cloth and accumulated junk of all kinds. Here beats the lively heart of Portloe. Leaning from the balcony of the small inn that almost literally overhangs the slipway, you may feast your eyes upon the scene, and inhale the composite aroma of seaweed, tar, paraffin, stale fish, lead paint, oilskins, old rope from dawn till dusk. Could you ask anything much better of life? It is to be doubted.

MELMERBY, Cumberland (*On A686, nine miles north-east of Penrith*).

This little village lies in the Vale of Eden, between the soaring Pennines to the east and the mountains of Lakeland to the west. If you approach it from the Pennines you will have dropped no less than 1,300 feet from a road summit squeezed between Black Fell and Fiends Fell—a road that was a mere mountain track until, a century or two ago, it was widened and surfaced to carry coaches between Penrith and Hexham by way of Alston, the highest market town in England. Here, though, it levels out to thread the village green, which falls like an apron from the single row of buildings above it: a delectable vision of russet-red Cumberland sandstone.

Prominent among them is one with a squat, castellated and louvered tower, with belfry and black-and-gold-faced clock. You would take it to be the church. In fact, it is the village schoolhouse, with the schoolmistress's residence attached. The church lies a hundred yards away, behind a stand of fine elms and a snug farmstead.

The very name Melmerby connotes serenity. But you have only to look eastwards to the escarpment from which you have just descended to realise that you are in an oasis set in wild country. You are looking at the rampart composed of Fiends Fell, Knock Fell, Dufton Fell and, greatest of them all, Cross Fell, almost 3,000 feet high. Off this rampart at certain seasons of the year there blows the notorious 'Helm Wind', whose effect has something in common with that of the mistral. In its deeper crevasses snow lies for ten months of the year—sometimes the whole year round. But as you relax here on the village green, in the dappled shade of the elms and limes and ash, you are unlikely to allow your thoughts to wander in that direction; for here, very truly, you find yourself in the blessed Vale of Eden.

WATENDLATH, Cumberland (*Between B5289 and A591, on a fell-side track*).

Only the larger-scale map gives any indication of a negotiable road to this Lilliputian hamlet on the side of its own tarn, squeezed between the heights of Brund and Armboth Fells. But do not expect a road. Rather, a winding, boulder-marked, steeply-climbing track cut through copses of beech, spruce and larch. After a while it emerges from the trees, between Lakeland stone walls, to peter out eventually at a hump-backed pack-horse bridge overlooked by a mere handful of slate-stone cottages. A beck from the tarn immediately beyond them spills among the smooth boulders beneath the bridge and on down the tight valley by which you have just climbed. You may have arrived by car ; it is very much more rewarding to have done these few miles on foot.

A superb panorama has now opened out about you. Here you are truly on top of the world. The fells climb away from you in all directions, split here and there by the narrow crevasses carved by tumbling becks for aeons past. You have entered a glorious amphitheatre of gently sloping, boulder-strewn, grey-green turf framing Watendlath Tarn. The clear water changes hue with changes in the sky, mirroring in its faintly ruffled surface the blue and snowy white of the scudding clouds.

Time here has hardly moved over the centuries; nor does it move today. You will soon adjust yourself to this welcome timelessness. The still tarn emphasises it. The only hint of movement is to be found in the musical tumbling of the beck beneath the bridge; before long it becomes part of the living silence of the place. May be the sheep tracks will set your feet tingling; more probably you will want just to relax for a day, a week, a month, while the minutes and hours drift imperceptibly by, their passage marked only by the alternating of darkness and dawn.

EYAM, Derbyshire (*Off A623, five miles north of Bakewell*).

A single street threads its way between the cottages of limestone and gritstone, roofed with the traditional heavy stone slabs, that constitute this north Derbyshire hamlet. Midway along it stands the parish church, largely Norman but built on a Saxon site and with Saxon relics in its fabric. Close to it stands a pleasant cottage with an ominous name: Plague Cottage. Here, just three centuries ago, the Great Plague of London reached Derbyshire in a parcel of clothing; and here the first of nearly three hundred inhabitants of this small community died.

Under the inspiring leadership of the Reverend William Mompesson, their rector, the people of Eyam voluntarily isolated themselves from the outside world for twelve months. Food was brought to them from neighbouring villages, deposited at one or other of a ring of stones at the self-imposed periphery half a mile from the centre of the plague-stricken village. The best known of these, a trickle of water rising between two stones, bears the name 'Mompesson's Well'; you may see it today, much as it was in 1665, when the villagers' coins were washed in the water and snatched up by the good folk of Grindleford whose offerings were thus paid for. You may see, too, the little dell in which Mompesson preached his weekly sermon, rather than crowd his flock into the church: Cucklett Church, the dell is now called, and on 'Plague Sunday' every year, the last Sunday in August, a commemorative service is still held in the dell. Mompesson's chair, the work of a local carpenter, today stands inside the church's chancel rails; gravestones in the churchyard are eloquent memorials, too.

But today the sun smiles over the dale in which the village lies, and the sky is filled with gliding enthusiasts from near by Hucklow: a contrast indeed.

34

OXENHAM ARMS, South Zeal, Devonshire (*Off A30, four miles east of Okehampton*).

This most famous inn lies in the heart of a hamlet nestling at the foot of the great Dartmoor landmark, Cawsand Beacon. Eight hundred years ago it was a lay monastery; having entered it, you may well feel that it is many centuries older than that. The impression you gain of antiquity is formidable, inescapable.

You will notice, set in the wall of a room on your left, a granite monolith similar to the many to be seen standing isolated on the high moors. Its foundations have been sought, but never located; archaeologists maintain that the house was in fact built round it. For eight centuries it has buttressed one of the inner walls. It is matched, incidentally, by another granite monolith that supports the massive beam spanning one of the great fireplaces.

Granite and oak, indeed—toughest and most enduring of raw materials—dominate the place; they are responsible for the pervading impression of solidity and strength. Enormous flagstones form the ground floors; the oak beams supporting the galleries and stairs, the upper floors and the framework of the inner walls, are all of heroic size; one fireplace consists of a granite block eight feet long by two feet thick supported on two shorter columns of similar girth: it could well be a medieval dungeon, but for the great fire that burns continuously within it. With so much massive and ancient stone about, it is not surprising that this inn is scheduled as an Ancient Monument. It even possesses a spiral stone staircase carved out of the thickness of an outside wall. It has held a license for nearly five centuries; and in its impressive forecourt two famous packs—the Eggesford and the Mid-Devon Fox-hounds—regularly meet, for here their territories adjoin.

YE OLDE MASONS ARMS, Branscombe, Devonshire (*On the coast, five miles east of Sidmouth*).

This most delectable village, lying at the foot of a steep valley that dips to the water's edge, possesses an atmosphere of tranquillity, and unity, rare even in a Devon village. It was Royal Property in King Alfred's day; it was 'awarded' to the Benedictine Monastery of St Peter in Exeter ten centuries ago; its church has a Norman tower; everything here bespeaks antiquity. And the inn itself is as old as the main fabric of the church; it is perfectly in keeping with the village as a whole. It is surrounded by small stone-built cottages no less old: cottages whose womenfolk for centuries have been famed for their pillow lace making—Queen Alexandra's wedding-dress had lace on it from the Branscombe pillows. Meanwhile the husbands occupied themselves less reputably with smuggling.

The inn clearly reveals its origin: a row of linked stone cottages descending to the foot of the hill. It is 'stepped' downwards and possesses three entrances, each crowned with a beehive thatched cone. A wide terrace forms a substantial plinth beneath the creeper-clad façade, and here you may sit at tables beneath more beehive thatched canopies and observe the leisured life of the village. The terrace is bordered by a low stone wall in which flowers grow all the year round in the mild, subtropical air. Within, the inn is cool in summer, warm on the rare cold winter days, for its walls of stone are two feet thick at least. Its ceilings are low on both floors, its fireplaces generously proportioned; through the deep window embrasures you may look out across the terrace at a signpost bearing the words: 'Now Ye Toil Not'. Plain statement, or advice offered? Whichever way you consider it, you will have little difficulty in accepting it.

CLOVELLY, Devonshire (*Off A39, ten miles west of Bideford*).

To ignore Clovelly would be to ignore a village that is unique of its kind in the whole country: it is the only village in which no wheeled vehicle is permitted, or indeed is practicable. It can only be penetrated on foot (or donkey-hoof). The only comprehensive view of it would be from a boat lying in the bay. From this you would step ashore on the little twisted quay encircling the sloping shingle beach beneath the three-centuries-old Red Lion Inn. (Formerly *The Red Lion and Jolly Sailor*, Charles Kingsley borrowed the name Salvation Yeo, in his novel *Westward Ho!*, from its one-time landlord.)

From the harbour, with its cluster of small fishing-boats, you make your way to the lower end of the single street. This is not even the right word, for this unique thoroughfare is a cross between a cobbled pathway and a somewhat flattened-out staircase. It climbs, in a length of about a quarter of a mile, no less than four hundred feet to the car park at the summit of the cliffs where (mercifully, in this age of petrol fumes and speed) all cars have had to be locked and left. So narrow is this thread-like street that from the casement windows of the lowly first floors it is almost possible for the occupants of the cottages to shake hands across your head. These shoulder-to-shoulder cottages are wedged into the steeply rising slopes that form the sides of this deep, narrow and precipitous cleft in the rock that tumbles to the bay; indeed, they give the impression, for all their whitewash and black paintwork, of having been quarried out of the rock on the opposing slopes. They have been for generations, for centuries, the homes of the hardy Devon fisher-folk, who still eke out a precarious living in stormy Bideford Bay.

WIDECOMBE-IN-THE-MOOR, Devonshire (*Three miles north of A384, five miles from Ashburton*).

Though this village stands some eight hundred feet above sea-level it is well named Widecombe 'in', rather than 'on' the Moor, for on all sides of it the turf-clad granite shoulders of Dartmoor swell upwards, sometimes to nearly twice that height. It nestles in a cup-like hollow, and to reach it you must descend steeply from every direction. Your beacon will be the great square tower of the Church of St Pancras, that thrusts upwards into the sky from the heart of the village like a lighthouse, a landmark for many miles around: it is small wonder that the church is known as The Cathedral of Dartmoor.

Hard by, in one of the two pleasant squares around which the cottages are grouped, stands The Church House, known also as The Sexton's Cottage: it is an impressive building composed of enormous granite blocks, important enough both architecturally and historically to have been designated National Trust property.

All is not harsh granite, however, in this smiling Dartmoor-in-Devon village, for ever linked in our minds with the saga of Uncle Tom Cobleigh and his Grey Mare. Indeed, here is an oasis among the granite tors, the dark, tumbling streams and the treacherous peat bogs of the Moor. Splendid chestnuts and sycamores grow in profusion on the wide green and at cottage corners, their roots serpentining among clefts in the rock; it is as though Mother Nature had determined to offer some compensation to a village doomed to lie at the heart of an otherwise hostile moorland, with the grim convict prison of Princetown but an hour's walk across the open moor. So, Widecombe lies like an uncut but glowing jewel in a setting so harsh that it serves only to emphasise its intrinsic beauty.

BRACE OF PHEASANTS, Plush, Dorset (*Just off B3143, eight miles north of Dorchester*).

Where else but in Dorset would you find a signpost directing you to 'Mappowder, Folly and Plush'? Follow the finger, down the twisting lane, to the last of the trilogy. Immediately in front of you, where the lane turns down to the diminutive stream, the Piddle, is the inn. Long and low, it was originally a brace of cottages, with a smithy at the far corner. It is stone walled, its upper windows half embedded in the heavy thatch; the façade bears the name, in flowing, glossy black lettering. There is also a unique inn sign: in a glass case slung from a wrought-iron bracket, a cock and hen pheasant, skilfully stuffed, are realistically perched: an almost living representation of the inn's name. Watch them attentively, and you will be ready to swear you saw a beady eye glint, a twitch of the splendid tail, a momentary shifting of claw grip on the bough. Adjacent to them hangs the oldest of all inn signs: a bunch of grapes that glows richly at night when the interior lamp is switched on.

Within, you find what you would expect. The long, low ceiling is supported by oak beams; these are unusually adorned with a fine array of racing-plates, each inscribed with its wearer's name, and the race he was entered for. Vertical beams are all that remains of the original parti-walls, affording a sense at once of space and comfort. A spiral staircase in one corner gives access to the tiny rooms upstairs.

You may wonder whether, in a hamlet embodying no more than some fifty persons, there could be any custom here. Raise the point at the bar, and you will be gently reminded that here, in this lost cranny of a county, there is a flourishing industry. Of what? Why, the growing and exporting of—orchids! Moreover, the telephone-kiosk and letter-box at the smithy corner bear the emblem of Queen Elizabeth II.

SMITHS ARMS, Godmanstone, Dorset (*On A352, four miles north of Dorchester*).

There is no argument: without question, this is the smallest of English inns. It stands hardly more than four feet high at its thatched eaves; it is barely ten feet across inside, and only a yard or so more in length from bar to door. Standing on the highway linking Sherborne with the Dorset coast it was, as the name suggests, originally a smithy that ministered to the needs of the waggon horses and pack-horse trains passing by. For two centuries or so it did this and nothing else. But one day in the mid-seventeenth-century King Charles II stopped there to have a horse's cast shoe replaced. Thirsty, he demanded a drink. The smith sadly confessed that he had no license. Whereupon the monarch promptly bestowed one upon him, and the smith turned smith-publican from that day on, to his own profit and the pleasure of his customers old and new.

You must stoop to pass under that conical thatched roof over the flint-faced cob walls. You find there is only one bar, though you are aware that licensed houses generally must by law have not less than two—Public and Saloon. A Royal Charter three centuries old permits the publican to 'break the law' with impunity, for King Charles had recognised the scantiness of the available accommodation.

Indeed, space is at a premium. A suspended cartwheel carries a rim-row of lamps. If you have your eyes on it when you sit down, you may find yourself impaled on the spreading horns of a Japanese water-buffalo, donated by an appreciative globe-trotting customer. Better, then, to relax in one of the array of former bus-seats that line the close-set walls and offer the maximum of comfort while occupying the minimum of space. But no longer will the publican be able to shoe your horse.

46

MILTON ABBAS, Dorset (*Just north of A354, five miles south-west of Blandford*).

If an adverse comment on this eighteenth-century village is possible—perish the thought!—then it is that even for a model village its uniformity, orderliness and symmetry are just a shade too perfect; indeed, almost overwhelming.

A single, wide street curves and rises gently, uniformly, throughout its length. It is bordered on each side by well-tended rectangles of greensward, each one bisected by a pathway leading to a cottage doorstep. Each cottage is identical with its neighbours: a central doorway, a window on either side of it, and three equally-spaced windows beneath generous eaves of thatch. Only the paint on the woodwork, relieving the cream-washed façades, is permitted a little individuality.

In the mid-eighteenth-century the first Earl of Dorchester, Lord of the Manor, decided that he no longer wished to be able to see the workers on his estate. He therefore built this village complete, to house them out of his sight. They lived sometimes three or four families to a cottage. Now, however, they are privately owned: desirable residences in a model village, complete with a church and a decorous inn at the top of the village—the only breaks in the uniformity. Once, a fine chestnut grew between each cottage and its neighbour; planted in the same year, they matured and became dangerous in the same year, and were recently felled. The saplings that have been planted in their stead will have to grow for several generations before they are capable of fulfilling the function of their predecessors. Meanwhile this quiet village—new among the ancient Dorset villages—remains an exemplar in stone and thatch of the precision and uniformity of the age that gave it birth.

KING'S HEAD, Chigwell, Essex (*On A113, ten miles north-east of London*).

This Elizabethan inn has been an important posting-house on the highway between East Anglia and London for most of its long life. During the reigns of Elizabeth I and James I the Forty Day Courts were held in a room now known as the 'Chester Room', a name deriving from its association with Charles Dickens. For in his novel, *Barnaby Rudge*, he named this inn *The Maypole*, and he set the famous encounter between Sir John Chester and Mr Haredale in this very room.

The inn has changed but little since those days, inside or out. The ground floor is faced with the typical Essex-style weather-boarding, interspersed with one or two square-cut bay windows and the twin white columns at the entrance. They help to support the overhanging upper floors of half-timbering inset with panels of plaster and lit by a variety of diamond-paned windows. Above these are five sharply pointed gables; they catch the eye today with their marked difference of size and proportion; they caught Dickens's observant eye a century and more ago: 'An old building (he wrote in his novel) with more gable ends than a lazy man would care to count; huge zigzag chimneys, out of which it seemed that even smoke could not choose to come in more than naturally fantastic shapes, imparted to it in its tortuous progress. . .'

Queen Elizabeth I, of course, slept here. It is said that she woke in a furious temper and boxed the ears of a groom who was clumsy in assisting her to mount her horse at the block beside the door. Dickens accepted the tradition; so may we! In a room where he spent much time there hangs on the wall a facsimile of a life insurance policy he took out when he was at the peak of his career as a popular novelist.

ROSE AND CROWN, Hempstead, Essex (*On B1054, five miles east of Saffron Walden*).

Until a century ago known as The Bell, this is the reputed birthplace in 1705 of Dick Turpin, highwayman. Certainly his father was landlord here, and his birth certificate hangs on the wall. Glance up at the low ceiling of the saloon bar and you will find a small hole cut in one of the oak beams. A hole cut in the floorboards of the room immediately above corresponds with this. The highwayman frequently took refuge here while on the run, and through this makeshift spyglass he was able to keep tabs on the men following his trail. Another reminder of the highwayman's connection with the inn may be seen on the mantelpiece. It is a statue of him on horseback, in fine Rockingham ware, donated to the inn 'in his memory'; a proviso states that it is to be preserved in its sealed glass case 'in perpetuity.' Well, why not? On the beam supporting it, inscribed in Gothic lettering, are the following lines:

LET MY CARE BE NO MAN'S SORROW;

PAY TODAY—AND TRUST TOMORROW!

Immediately facing the inn, across the road, is a circle of eight Dutch elms, survivors of the original twelve, estimated to be three hundred years old. Linked by a double row of heavy chains, they formed a thirty-foot circular cockpit. Cock-fighting, happily, is a thing of the past (though whispers of its survival in remote places are occasionally heard); a Methodist chapel today overlooks the grisly site. Behind the inn, a century before the highwayman was born, William Harvey, discoverer of the circulation of the blood, first saw light. His family were the owners of the inn. He, and the rascal who was hanged for his crimes at the age of thirty-four, vie with one another as Hempstead's most famous sons.

FINCHINGFIELD, Essex (*On B1053, nine miles north of Braintree*).

Two small roads peel off the main Saffron Walden-Braintree road and dip towards an expanse of water. They do not merely enclose a triangular village green, they take the eye and lead it down to the narrow hump-backed bridge of mellow brick that temporarily unites them on one side of the village pond. Then they diverge: one to bear left, passing on its way a white-painted, weather-boarded post-mill, the other to sweep rightwards and vanish beneath the squat flint and stone tower of the Church of St John the Baptist, in the fair heart of the village.

This blend of gentle curve and clearly defined triangle as the two roads swing across the green to unite at the bridge is wholly satisfying to the eye. It contributes notably to the dominant impression you receive of orderliness and symmetry, not imposed from without upon the scene but deriving from the fact that this village has been laid out upon a falling slope.

But now cross the modest bridge. Facing you, a causeway links post-mill and church. Above it, a terrace of gabled cottages with small dormer windows confronts you. There is some thatch, but in the main roofs are of dark red and russet tiles above white and cream-washed façades broken by small, well proportioned mullioned windows. From these you would look down across the sloping green apron to the swans cruising on the pond; or sideways at the beautiful wrought-iron bracket carrying the signboard of The Green Man. Beyond that, the church, with its memorial to William Kemp, who preserved a self-imposed silence for seven years. He knew what he was doing; his gesture was in keeping with the serenity of the village in which he had had the good sense to make his home.

54

NEWPORT, Essex (*On A11, sixteen miles south of Cambridge*).

Glance to your left as you approach from the north. Curiously inset in a wall are pieces of carved stone; facing them, a chest-high, hollowed-out stone block. On this, in medieval times, food was placed for the inmates of the leper hospital set back among the willows on the river bank. Lepers and hospital have gone; only these relics remain. Just beyond them, bear left off the main road, to follow the old road, Bridge End. In one stride you pass from the twentieth-century into another, more gracious, age.

A row of pollarded limes at once catches your eye; and, half screened by them, a row of pleasingly variegated houses, each a 'character' in its own right. They stand shoulder to shoulder, as they have done for centuries: ancient half-timbering, heavy Essex-style weather-boarding, façades of flint, brick and stone. One house offers a fine example of the 'shell' porch, bearing the date 1692. Known as The Crown House, it reminds you that Charles II owned property hereabouts. Its façade is notable for the unusually large leaded panes, and for specimens of pargetting second only in quality to that of neighbouring Suffolk. A glance through those panes reveals some impressive oak wainscotting.

The pearl of this old street, however, lies at its lower end, near the bridge. Here is *The Old Three Tuns*. It ceased to be an inn within the lifetime of older Newport folk; but it still carries the wrought-iron sign bracket—a beautiful example of the blacksmith's craft. If you are privileged to enter the house you will find that the new owners have skilfully and imaginatively retained the layout and atmosphere of the former inn while making it into a home for themselves.

THE LAMB INN, Filkins, Gloucestershire (*On A361, four miles south of Burford*).

This centuries-old inn is remarkable for possessing one of the finest Stonesfield slate roofs in a county outstanding for such fine roofs. Its Cotswold stonework is almost completely covered by luxuriant creeper, through which the windows peep almost as though through thatch. It faces a stand of chestnuts on a diminutive green, offering a welcome to one of the less well-known villages of the district, still quite unspoiled, and an inducement, too, to linger within its homely walls.

The bars are noteworthy for one of the finest collection of straw, or corn, 'dollies' you are likely to find the length and breadth of the country; they are all the work of a local craftsman, practitioner of a craft now sadly dying out; and they are remarkable for their diversity of subject. Here are the traditional patterns, of course; but also such unusual objects as a shepherd's crook and, most striking of all, a beautifully fashioned ship's anchor and stock. Beautiful in themselves, they are also a reminder that the original customers here were not visitors but local men who lived and worked on farms and in quarries within a stone's throw of this doorstep. Other relics here are two 'Cricketers Plates' of Worcester porcelain bearing the signatures of Australian touring sides, and some 'fire plaques'—reminders of the days when such objects were seen on outer walls as testimony of insurance.

Behind the inn are the stone-built cottages of a village notable for its uniformity of architectural style. The dividing-walls consist, strangely, of great slabs of stone set on edge, on which fossil markings make arresting patterns. One of the cottages houses a museum of objects of local interest well worth a lingering visit, for it shows at a glance how traditions have been maintained in this unspoiled corner.

THE RED LION, Northleach, Gloucestershire (*On A40, nine miles west of Burford*).

Four centuries ago, when this inn was built, Northleach was one of the great Cotswold 'Wool Towns'. Its fine buildings, its almshouses, above all its great church, with its magnificent tower and a South Porch held by many connoisseurs to be the finest example of the Perpendicular style in England, provide evidence of this, though now its heyday is but a memory. It stands at the junction of two important highways: that from Gloucester to London, and the famous Roman Fosse Way which runs a hundred and sixty miles from the English Channel to the North Sea at Flamborough Head and is never more than six miles out of dead-straight throughout its whole length. Packhorse-trains and bagmen, coaches and wool-wains, travelling north, south, east or west, passed this way; and if they stayed overnight, then they put up at this coaching inn. Four hundred years old, it is a beautiful example of an over-hanging half-timbered upper storey superimposed upon a ground floor built of local stone, and the whole is spanned by a steeply pitched roof of exquisitely graduated Cotswold slate.

You enter it by way of a door set in the archway to the right, through which in days gone by the waggons and the horses that drew them, the waggoners, coachmen and postilions passed to the stables at the rear. As you duck beneath the lintel, and beneath the ancient beams supporting the ceilings within, you may be forcibly reminded that when masons and carpenters began work on this inn men were generally smaller in stature than they are today. From the upper windows you look across the sloping square, lined with stone buildings erected in an age when men built them to last, and paid for them with money earned from the sale of wool far and wide: merchants who took refreshment, and slept, beneath the roof of this fine old Cotswold inn.

60

BIBURY, Gloucestershire (*On A433, midway between Cirencester and Burford*).

Spacious, shallow, crystal clear, fed by a dozen unseen springs, the Coln flows leisurely through the heart of this most beautiful village of Cotswold stone. One of the delights of lingering here is to watch the innumerable young trout darting over the green weed that forms the velvet bottom of the stream. They are bred in their thousands in Bibury for the re-stocking of Yorkshire trout streams.

But your eyes will soon lift, as they must always do in this incomparable region of oolitic limestone, to the buildings all about you: the gracious Swan Hotel, with its smooth lawns dotted among the trout-hatching pools; the ancient buttressed corn mill above the bridge; the scattered cottages large and small nestling beneath the hanging woods. Above all, to the sloping terrace of ancient cottages, National Trust property, now, and therefore safe for perpetuity, Arlington Row, Bibury's most treasured possession.

Each of the nine linked cottages, hardly larger than dolls' houses, has its own numbered door; guttering and woodwork are painted a delicate blue as a foil to the grey stone; a dozen chimneys rise from the long stone-slab roof, and as many gables large and small, and dormer windows to match. Creepers mask windows so small that you would think only dwarfs could see through them. They would peer out across a glinting streamlet dipping past the thresholds of their doors to the Coln beyond the green and the small trout shuttling through the green woof beneath.

Beyond lies the main road that brought you here and by which you will leave the village. Traffic passes leisurely along it: who would be so foolish as to hurry through the enchantment that is Bibury?

SNOWSHILL, Gloucestershire (*Off A44, three miles south of Broadway*).

The village lies in a tight fold of limestone particularly generously endowed with trees. If you are not on the alert you may well miss it altogether, for the trees invade the village on all sides and you could well fail to realize that it was there among them at all. Moreover, it lies on no main or even secondary road, but on a lane forking off another lane that darts suddenly down into it, turns an abrupt angle and departs as swiftly as it arrived.

Your best view of it is looking down on it from one of the few gaps among the trees. Only from this vantage-point can you see it as a whole: a cluster of buildings the majority of which are small (though there is the sixteenth-century Manor House high on the crest of the opposing hill), terraced on three sides of the Church of St Barnabas which, oddly enough, occupies a part of the slanting village green. The cottages rise upwards and away from the church, but in a lingering fashion, as though contentedly tied to its green apron-strings: the majority of them are older by several centuries than the church itself, which is relatively modern, but a century old.

When you have savoured to the full this bird's-eye view of the village, take the right fork and drop quickly down into its heart. Now the tree-clad slopes rise on all sides, away from you, emphasizing the seclusion of the village. You will notice that there are hardly two roofs on the same level, hardly two façades in the same line. You will notice too, close by the church, a length of high wall of Cotswold stone in traditional style, into which have been inset a number of oddly shaped and variegated lumps of stone. These catch the sunlight in a subtle fashion and imbue the whole length of wall with a curiously attractive sense of movement.

THE FOX & HOUNDS, Beauworth, Hampshire (*Just off A272, five miles east of Winchester*).

It is to be found on the crest of a tree-shaded hill just outside a small hamlet that lies near the main road to Winchester. A flint-and-brick wall encloses lawn and garden overlooked by the windows of this cottage-type inn which is tile-hung almost to the ground. Unpretentious exteriorly, and looking more like a private residence than a public house, it conceals many centuries of history. They are represented by the well behind the saloon bar and the unique tread-wheel mounted on an enormous oak shaft above it. Twelve feet in diameter, with eight massive oaken spokes, it is wide enough for two men to operate it side by side. When beer was brewed here, a donkey and donkey-man were permanently housed and employed beneath this roof. The well is three hundred feet deep; a man, or donkey, has to 'walk' nearly half a mile every time water is fetched in that massive iron-hooped, eighteen-gallon barrel.

It was not sunk for the inn. Archaeologists state that it served the occupants of a castle built in King Stephen's reign, and the present inn was built round it on the castle's site. The water—crystal-clear and ice-cold—has never been known to fail. Legend, of course, has accumulated about the well. King Stephen, it is said, hid his treasures in it. Whether this is so hardly matters today. When you stand by it, the centuries drop away. The massive refectory table at which you eat, worn smooth by long use, is less old than the well. If you are invited to drum your heel on the oaken lid you will hear the reverberations echoing thunderously beneath you, dying to a distant murmur in the solid rock; they are re-iterating, as it were, the moments of history long past; as you listen to them, it is not difficult to find yourself slipping backwards in time, as the barrel slips silently down to the water.

66

THE MASTER BUILDERS HOUSE, Buckler's Hard, Hampshire
(Off B3054, ten miles south of Southampton).

An inn? It looks more like a Georgian private house. And that, in fact, is what it was when it was built some two and a half centuries ago. It is the last of a row of mellow brick buildings that slope down to the edge of the Beaulieu River, within a mile or two of the Solent. Facing them across a wide gravel road is a similar row, the uppermost of which used to be the inn. The hamlet was established in the early eighteenth-century for the sole purpose of housing the workers employed on building ships for the Royal Navy. On the slipway were stored enormous numbers of oak trees felled in the near-by New Forest to supply timbers and planking. Over-all command of the shipwrights was in the hands of the great Henry Adams, master-shipwright, who designed and built such famous ships as the 64-gun *H.M.S. Agamemnon* and the 74-gun *H.M.S. Swiftsure*. He lived and worked in this house, which has now taken his name.

You will find in it not only the great fireplaces and massive beams that give it character, but also the room with the great window overlooking the 'hard' and the estuary, from which he could keep an eye on the progress of the ship building for which he was responsible; the great window threw ample light on the table on which he laid out his plans for the men-o'-war commissioned from him by the Admiralty. Many of them were in action at the Battle of Trafalgar. He lived to be nearly a hundred, and after his death in 1805 his son and nephew continued his great tradition.

Now there is no more shipbuilding, here. But from his window you can look out across the water at the yachts and smaller boats threading the channels. And in the old inn, now a museum of local interest, you will find yourself surrounded by relics of the century during which the master builder and his shipwrights flourished.

THE
MASTER BUILDERS HOUSE
FULLY   LICENSED

NEW INN, Pembridge, Herefordshire (*On A44, seven miles west of Leominster*).

This half-timbered inn, with its twin projecting gables and cobbled terrace must be at least five hundred years old. Known for centuries, oddly enough, as 'The Inn Without a Name', it was a stopping-place for travellers between London and the Welsh coast; today it is mainly visited by people in search of the picturesque that is truly genuine.

Few inns today give any indication of their importance in coaching days, apart from a spacious courtyard and a mounting-block or two. Here, however, it would be difficult to forget that horse-drawn coaches were regular callers. You eat, for example, in what was originally the stable. For convenience, some of the oak beams that separated stall from stall have been removed; others remain, to induce a sense of privacy. On the massive walls are the curved iron mangers from which the horses drew their fodder; they are kept filled with sweet-smelling hay, the scent of which delicately pervades the air all about you. The old cowsheds—for this was farm as well as hostelry—are now the up-to-date kitchens.

Farm and hostelry, and Court Room too, in olden times. The magistrates dispensed rough justice here, and it is believed that the Treaty which ended the Wars of the Roses was signed in this room. Pembridge was important, once, for its Wool Market. It stands immediately outside the door of the inn: a many-pillared edifice beneath whose roof buyers and sellers met and haggled. One pillar is mounted on a stone plinth, the 'Preachers' Stone', where itinerant evangelists preached the Faith: all this beneath the shadow cast by the gables of this most inappropriately named 'New' inn, a centre of many activities for many centuries past.

DILWYN, Herefordshire (*On A4112, three miles north of Weobley*).

What there is of this diminutive hamlet lies along a short rising stretch of road between two dog's-leg turns. Your eye will certainly be arrested by the porches of two half-timbered cottages that are in striking contrast to the modesty of their main fabric. They are in fact constructed of fine moulded oak beams taken from the church long ago when it was being restored. There are other relics of the church now in new settings here: for example, some fine panelling to be seen in the *Crown Inn*, which stands at the foot of the hill where the second dog's-leg marks the end of the village and the beginning of open pastureland once more.

The Church of St Mary the Virgin, standing on a tree-shaded knoll overlooking the corner, dominates this handful of cottages. A beautifully proportioned octagonal spire, roofed with cedar shingles, springs from the squat twelfth-century tower, which contains a ring of six bells more than two hundred years old. They are worth a close look. One of them you will find is inscribed with the sobering statement: 'I To The Church The Living Call; And To The Grave Do Summon ALL.'

Not so long ago there was a curious structure at the entrance to the church, called The Scanniels. It contained a six-foot water-wheel with massive spokes 'That will turn SPITTS, 2 CHURNS, and BEAT in a MORTER', as the original notice read. Here is an echo of the day-to-day life of a hamlet that seems hardly to have grown over the years and today maintains a resolute air of withdrawnness. Yet it knew tempestuous times. In a farmstead near by is an enclosure which this community, like others on the Welsh border, used to secure its cattle and womenfolk from the fiery invaders making their swift forays across the line of the Mercian King Offa's Dyke.

YE OLD FIGHTING COCKS, St Albans, Hertfordshire (*On the south side of the city*).

In a creditable attempt to justify its claim to be 'the oldest inhabited licensed house in Britain', a signboard declares that it was 're-built after the Flood'. So it was; but the 'Flood' was the overflowing of the Ver (St Albans was formerly Verulamium) some centuries ago, and the building stands on this little river's bank. There is, however, no question as to its great antiquity. Originally a medieval dove-cote, it was re-erected on its present site nearly five centuries ago, given a tall, buttressed chimney, and re-named 'The Rounde House'. Its site was the water-gate of the neighbouring Abbey; here the monks kept their boat and their fishing-tackle; here they received the bodies of monks who had died at the Benedictine Priory at Redbourn, a few miles distant, when they were brought to St Albans for interment in the Abbey Cemetery.

Came the Dissolution of the Monasteries; The Rounde House—which was, and is, in fact octagonal rather than circular in plan—became an inn. Its shape, and its situation, commended itself to the devotees of what was then Britain's most popular sport: its central room was furnished as a cock-pit, and the appropriate name bestowed upon the inn. It remained a centre for cock-fighting for centuries.

If, as is claimed, its foundation goes back to 795 A.D., then its earliest 'inhabitants' must have been pigeons; but in one form or another it has certainly stood for six, seven, perhaps eight centuries. For much of the time it had the protection of the Abbey; look out from its windows, and you see the original monks' pond, from which they extracted their fish; from the main bar you look into the former cock-pit; in one of its heavily timbered chambers Oliver Cromwell, who frequently slept here, was wont to stable his horse; the Abbey of St Alban towers above you still.

74

ALDBURY, Hertfordshire (*Off A41, four miles east of Tring*).

This place will satisfy the seeker after the 'perfect' village. Its centre is an oval pond of clear water set like a jewel in the heart of a triangular green; on the green stand the old stocks and whipping-post; overhanging it is a venerable elm of enormous girth. And overlooking the green on all three sides are cottages three centuries old and more. Some of them are lattice-windowed almshouses. Alongside them stands the gem of them all: a beautifully preserved manor-house nearly four hundred years old whose ornate brickwork is set in noble half-timbering; it has one magnificent gable, and chimneys of distinction, and its latticed windows look down upon the green.

In the garden of a row of linked cottages stands a curious brick structure which, upon inspection, proves to be at once well-house, bake-house and village wash-house. You may examine the bake-ovens and great coppers, set in the thickness of the walls, and the sixty-foot well beneath the old-fashioned wheel-pump. Once each group of cottages possessed this amenity; now, but one of them remains.

Set on a slight eminence overlooking the peaceful green and the cottages lining the three little roads that converge upon it, stands the thirteenth-century Church of St John the Baptist, built of local flint and stone. You step down into it: the step down symbolising, as is often the case with churches of St John's name, the descent into water at the time of baptism. Immediately inside the south door you will find a narrow flight of stone steps twisting upwards into a 'parvise', a small room built over the porch and probably used by visitors to the neighbouring Priory of Missenden. From the churchyard you look across the village to the monument to the Duke of Bridgewater, erected on the Chiltern spur beneath which the village lies, virtually unchanged.

THE LION, Buckden, Huntingdonshire (*Off A1, four miles south of Huntingdon*).

The little village of Buckden is now by-passed by the newly aligned Great North Road; but it is worth turning aside for as you speed north or south some sixty miles north of London. Half hidden beneath overshadowing trees you will see a fine wall of ancient mellow brick; behind it lie the ruins of Buckden Palace, official residence of the Bishops of Lincoln six centuries ago. At the end of the wall stands an inn which was originally the Palace Guest House; in the great days of the coaches (and highwaymen) it became one of the most famous of the posting-houses that studded the highway between London and York and beyond.

Perhaps the most convincing evidence of its early ecclesiastical associations may be found in a carved oak boss forming the hub of a 'wheel' of moulded beams supporting the ceiling of the original kitchen, with its chamfered chimney-beam of ten-foot span and carved rose decorations: this boss is of undisputed fifteenth-century craftsmanship. It depicts the traditional emblem of Lamb and Pennant; and in fact for most of its long life this inn has been known either as *The Lamb* or as *The Lamb & Flag*, only acquiring its present name, or its alternative, *The Lion & Lamb*, in the last hundred years or so. The symbol is surrounded by the words 'Ecce Agnus Dei', 'Behold the Lamb of God', and modestly decorated with a spray of four exquisitely carved leaves.

As is so often the case, the sense of antiquity is stronger within than without; you are aware of it immediately you enter. The 'ghost' of the Bishops' Palace is near by; the old fish-ponds, linked with its moat, in which carp were bred for the table, may be seen behind the inn; a slope of ground towards you is still known as the Palace 'Vineyard'. It was well worth momentarily leaving the main road.

HEMINGFORD GREY, Huntingdonshire (*Just north of A604, four miles east of Huntingdon*).

Twin villages, Hemingford Abbots and Hemingford Grey, lie within a stone's throw of one another, on the south bank of the Ouse. You may take your pick between them, for both are well worth a visit.

Make first for the river. You turn a corner at the dead-end of a narrow street and are perhaps surprised to find that the parish church is not, as is usually the case, in the heart of the village, or on a rise dominating it; here it stands right on the water's edge. The ancient Church of St James, with its noble tower and curiously truncated spire, seems almost to rise out of the placid waters that so beautifully reflect it; if you were so minded, you could dive off a gravestone into them; you may hire a boat from the boatyard alongside the graveyard.

Close behind the church, embowered by trees, is the Manor House. Dating from the twelfth-century, it can boldly claim to be among the most ancient in the country. Clustering about it, and the church, but, as it were, keeping their respectful distance, are wattle-and-daub cottages washed in warm cream and near-pink; they have snug thatched roofs, from which the upper windows peep out as beneath drawn eyebrows, scanning the river, the boats, and the once all-important corn mill.

There is some half-timbering here—which is surprising in a region not particularly noted for this style of building. And as you wander about the narrow street and the little lanes that branch off it, you will notice that many of the cottages bear names containing 'Glebe' or 'Grey': you will not be far wrong in conjecturing that they had ecclesiastical or noble historical associations in years gone by.

THE LEATHER BOTTLE, Cobham, Kent (*On B2009, four miles west of Rochester*).

'Any letter addressed to me at The Leather Bottle, Cobham, will be forwarded—supposing I still exist. Life, my dear Pickwick, has become insupportable to me. You may tell Rachel—Ah, that name!' So wrote Mr Tracy Tupman after his amatory disappointment.

You must look keenly for the object that gives this ancient inn its name. Above the crooked oak timbers, the cob-and-plaster in-filling, the diamond-paned leaded windows with their occasional bottle-base insets, and below the tiled roof, hangs the famous sign: Mr Pickwick, G.C.M.P.C., stands on a chair, his left hand concealed beneath his coat tail, characteristically declaiming. Above the signboard is a replica of an old-time leather water-bottle; the original, discovered by chance many years ago, filled with golden sovereigns, may still be seen in the dining-room.

Not surprisingly, the whole place is redolent of Dickens and his creations. A plaque depicting him crowns the main entrance; the walls of every bar, the dining-room, lounges and corridors are literally covered with framed sketches—many of them originals—depicting the wealth of characters and episodes from the novels.

Built more than three centuries ago, it has outlived the violence of Royalists and Roundheads, and stood firm under the battering of more recent and terrible weapons. It is for its Dickensian associations above all else that it stands today. When you have steeped yourself in its atmosphere, cross the road to a church possessing some of the finest brasses in England; take a look, too, at Cobham Hall, home for centuries of the great Darnley family, and the acres of flowers in Cobham Park: all this within a stone's throw of the inn.

RAMBLERS REST, Chislehurst, Kent (*Off A208, ten miles south-east of London*).

It may surprise you to find an inn so rural in appearance, and bearing such a name, barely ten miles from the heart of London. You will have to make a little effort to locate it, but the effort will prove well worth while, for here is an oasis of quiet almost within earshot of busy main roads, a place where the man or woman still happy to use Shanks's Mare will feel truly at ease. Though not ten miles from London, it is in a truly rural setting: trees fill the green sloping up and away from it; you have only to cross the road, and you are in silver birch country, among the 'white ladies of the forest'.

Its style is unusual, too, so close to the metropolis: white-painted weather-boarding. It is so small that it gives the impression of being an overgrown dolls' house. The impression is changed when you enter the diminutive porch and step down into the bar. It proves to be one of those odd buildings that are apparently larger inside than out. Clearly it was once just a cottage. This, though, was some three hundred years ago, and the building has possessed a licence for two hundred years. When you walk down those few steps you pass out of lightness into shade; the white paint of the exterior, and the sunshine, have given place to oak beams and artificial lighting, for in the bar you are below ground level and the windows are small. Another room is in sight, reached down more steps, for the inn is built on a steep slope and its builder adjusted his design to the conditions imposed on him.

The arrangement makes for snugness and companionship. Clearly this is a favourite haunt, with the personal touch. Unusual—perhaps unique—evidence of the fact is to be seen in the extraordinarily varied collection of decorative silk ties, every one of which was autographed by the owner before being presented to the inn.

PENSHURST, Kent (*On B2188, four miles west of Tonbridge*).

Strictly, perhaps, this small Kentish village lying at the confluence of the stripling Medway and the Eden, is but an appendage of the 'Great House', Penshurst Place. Yet, historically important as the Great House is, this village, with its old smithy, its handful of cottages and shops, is a charmer in its own right. And without doubt the most charming feature is its 'Leicester Square': a modest square indeed when contrasted with its opposite number in London. A wide, shallow flight of steps leads to a small expanse girded on three sides by late-fifteenth-century half-timbered and tile-hung buildings, one of which now houses the post-office; above them, tall chimneys, beautifully moulded, reach for the sky. On the far side, a low-beamed archway, supported by timbers, gives access to the churchyard of the church whose origins date back to the early thirteenth-century—older, in fact, than the original building of Penshurst Place, the splendid pile whose walls rise from the greensward beyond it.

Here Sir Philip Sidney, soldier, poet, courtier, scholar, was born a decade before Shakespeare, yet the great house was already two centuries old. Why does one approach it by way of Leicester Square? Because the Earl of Leicester was Sir Philip's uncle. His heirs succeeded to the property. Today it is still occupied by one of his descendants, Viscount de L'Isle and Dudley, V.C. You are at liberty to wander through the gardens, the Great Hall, the State Rooms, at your leisure. But leave yourself nevertheless sufficient time to linger a while in the homelier setting of the square by which you approached Penshurst Place. For this is the heart of the village; here you may absorb its flavour, meet the villagers, who go about their ordinary ways, hardly conscious, in all probability, of the glory that is theirs.

DOWNHAM, Lancashire (*One mile east of A59, three miles north of Clitheroe*).

Not ten miles from busy cotton towns, as the chough flies, this hamlet is the living witness that Lancashire is not 'all industrial'. Pendle Hill rises to the south-west.

Cross Downham Beck by the small stone bridge and slowly climb the street towards the tree-clad summit dominated by the sixteenth-century Church of St Leonard (patron-saint of prisoners) and *The Assheton Arms*, with its sign: 'Nec Arrogo Nec Dubito'. But take your time, for each yard of this mounting street should halt you in your tracks. Here is stone architecture-in-miniature. Every cottage is beautifully proportioned, matched with its neighbour, with a low-pitched roof of heavy stone slabs and a stone-slab footbridge to the door across the stone-cut gully flanking the street. The doorways, though, are unexpectedly large. The explanation is that until not so long ago, hand-loom weaving was carried on in these cottages, and the doorways had to be large enough to permit the passage of the looms.

But the outstanding building is The Old Well House, just opposite. A projecting two-storey porch with a Norman arch surmounting a square-hewn door breaks the line of mullioned windows whose lights are in groups of three, four and five, all small paned. Until the other day, the well-head, now blocked up, filled the crook of the porch. The house is designated as of Historic and Architectural Interest.

At the top of the hill, turn about. Is not the view downhill even more alluring than that from the bridge at its foot? But you have turned your back on one of Downham's most attractive features: a convex terrace of five cottages set above a sloping lawn between church and inn, each with a differently painted door to emphasize the cool beauty of the local stone, of which the whole trim village from bridge to church is built.

88

FERRY INN, Horning, Norfolk (*Off B1354, ten miles north-east of Norwich*).

The village of Horning lies on the Bure, one of a number of intersecting streams and small rivers that, with the score and more of lakes of varying size, comprise 'The Broads' and offer the enthusiast some two hundred miles of inland yachting and motor-cruising. It is one of the most popular rendezvous of the whole sprawling network of waterways; and without question its focal point is this yachtsmen's inn. White-painted walls above a black-painted brick plinth surmounted by half-timbering and thickly thatched, it looks out across spacious lawns dotted with sunshades from beneath which you leisurely contemplate the kaleidoscopically changing scene of yachts, launches, dinghies and their cheerful crews. Its great circular bow-window is an admirable 'grandstand'.

The inn makes no claim to antiquity, historical or literary associations; enough that it is a yachtsman's paradise! Moored alongside its river frontage, stem to stern, are the yachts and cabin-cruisers large and small, owned or hired by enthusiasts whose hobby is fresh-water sailing, inland. The whole district is unique. Mast tips appear among the tree-tops: they are cruising along the network of waterways that link Horning with Wroxham, Acle, Potter Heigham and the rest of those delectable yachtsmen's ports-of-call. But they will go far before they find an inn better sited than this one, at the ferry across the Bure, which operates from the edge of the lawn.

You can eat, drink and relax here most of the year round, and in the best of company. In winter the boats are laid up, but your company may then well be that of long-distance skaters. And of course bird sanctuaries abound among The Broads. So, it is small wonder that this unassuming inn attracts so many people of so many tastes: it has so much to offer them, the whole year round.

LITTLE WALSINGHAM, Norfolk (*Off B1105, four miles north of Fakenham*).

Your first hint that you are approaching an unusually interesting village is when you come to the Slipper Chapel. Why the odd name, you wonder. Inquiries reveal that in past centuries the devout making pilgrimage to the Shrine of Our Lady of Walsingham halted here to doff their footgear in order to make the last mile barefoot. You follow their route along a narrow, hedge-bordered lane, to reach the foot of a narrow street up which thousands of pilgrims have walked. On either side are half-timbered buildings, flint and stone gateways, hints of ancient treasure behind high stone walls. The road opens out into a little square at the top. You have just passed on your right the massive gateway to the Augustinian Priory; behind it is the site of a thousand-year-old shrine; near by, the pair of holy wells alongside which the virtuous Lady of the Manor, Richeldis, inspired by a visitation from the Holy Mother of God, erected a chapel. Confronting you in the square, backed by ancient buildings, is the 'Conduit House', the octagonal village pump-house at which the exhausted pilgrims slaked their thirst. Oddly, it bears on its summit a brazier in which a beacon can be lit.

Now all about you are relics of 'England's Nazareth, the Holy Land of Walsingham': the site of the Leper Hospital, the Martyrs' Field, the pilgrims' guest-houses, the ruins of a Franciscan Friary. You are made aware that you are not only in a historic place but in the heart of a place that has been a magnet drawing the devout for centuries; indeed, it does so still. Pilgrimages are still made, today; but the Shrine of Our Lady of Walsingham is now in the Slipper Chapel, so the pilgrimage is made, as it were, in reverse. Nevertheless, the setting remains much as it has always been, and you will quickly become imbued with its powerful atmosphere.

WOODBASTWICK, Norfolk (*Off A1151, in Broadland, north-east of Norwich*).

This surely merits the title, The Perfect Village? It is entirely integrated. Its centre is a triangular green, beautifully kept. On it stands the village pump, housed in an octagonal brick and stone wall surmounted by oak posts carrying a conical roof, reed thatched. Look about you in any direction. All the cottages are of red brick, some of them half-timbered; all have well-kept gardens. In one of them lives the blacksmith, in another the water-bailiff, in another the gamekeeper, in another the forester; and so on. Just beyond the green, shyly retiring behind a spread of magnificent chestnuts, is the flint-and-stone Church of St Fabian and St Sebastian, some parts of it six centuries old. Its tower overtops the tallest trees; but when you approach it you will not be surprised to find that its main structure is roofed—with thatch. No county in England has finer reed thatching than Norfolk; and you will look far in this county for finer examples of reed thatching than you see here.

Perhaps you are puzzled by this predominating impression of uniformity in this hamlet tucked away on the edge of the Broads, remote from main and secondary roads. The explanation lies in the fact that this is, in the best sense, a 'private' village. The villagers are all, one way and another, in the employ of 'the Big House', lying remote among its splendid trees overlooking the water. A benevolent squire, one would imagine: for here is an atmosphere of peace and contentment, epitomised by the last house you see as you leave the village. It is an alms-house. On an oak beam carrying the gable is painted the legend: 'At Evening Time It Shall Be Light . An aged retainer lives modestly there in the evening of his days, untroubled; in such a setting those poetic words take on a special significance.

94

THE BOAT, Stoke Bruerne, Northamptonshire (*Off A508, three miles east of Towcester*).

This thatched, local-stone-built inn was here long before the old Grand Junction (now the Grand Union) Canal was excavated by the 'navvies' who got their name from the large-scale 'navigations' of their era. It is one of the few surviving canal-side inns; generations of narrow-boatmen have tied up here, baited their horses in the stables that are part of the building, drunk the strong beer formerly brewed beneath its roof, and stocked up their boats' larders with good red meat from the butchery that was an important part of the inn. There are boatmen alive today who remember doing so. One family has managed the inn for nearly a hundred years.

Today it is both inn and museum. You will see on an outside wall one of the old Fire Insurance plaques—comparatively rare today. Inside, you will find a century-old table of red oak which used to be mounted on a swivel until customers protested that their beer mugs were being emptied by centrifugal motion! You will find, too, many fine specimens of the boldly painted, traditional metalware, ornamented with Castle and Rose, without which no self-respecting narrow-boatman would travel the canals; their counterparts are still to be seen on the few surviving boats and butties that continue to ply north and south.

These lovingly collected specimens sufficiently whet the appetite for a very remarkable Museum of Canal Transport to be found just across the locks, in a former warehouse, organised most imaginatively by British Waterways. To linger here, on either side of the canal, among these fascinating relics, is to find oneself slipping back in time to an age when industrial history was in the making; and to be keenly conscious of the ghosts of those legions of tough men who helped to make it.

ALWINTON, Northumberland (*On the southern slopes of Cheviot, ten miles north-west of Rothbury*).

You approach this hamlet over a road dressed with red granite chippings, offering a pleasant contrast to the rich green of the water-meadows. As you arrive, a striking sign reminds you that you are in the heart of Northumbria's National Park. Here, beneath a modest bridge, the Coquet and the Alwin, having tumbled off the slopes of the hills that are the hamlet's backcloth, merge, to continue on their way. You can take in the whole of this place in one swift glance: a cottage or two fronting the green, post-office, village shop, and the massive little inn. This is aptly named the Rose & Thistle—for but a mile or two away England and Scotland meet on the skyline.

The only road out of Alwinton to the north is clearly and emphatically marked: 'No Through Road'. You may drive a mile or two along it; then it peters out in a farmyard. Thereafter, you must walk, following the zigzagging course of the little Coquet that continually sub-divides, leaving you with a bewildering choice of sheep-tracks as you make for 'the end of it all', shown on your map in Latin: 'Ad Fines'. Here the Roman legions had their most northerly camp, on a site more desolate, and certainly less picturesque, than the village you have left behind you, but which is still within view. Here, half buried in the shaggy turf, are the mysteriously named Outer and Middle Golden Pots. Map in hand, you may try to locate them. A triumph, if you succeed! But whether you do or not, there is now the exhilarating walk down the undulating slopes alongside the beck to the shelter and refreshment awaiting you within the massive stone walls of Alwinton's little inn. Here, in the heart of a tiny, isolated community, you are in an oasis of peace, at the foot of those turbulent, deserted hill slopes where history was made two thousand years ago.

YE OLDE TRIP TO JERUSALEM, Nottingham (*On the west side of the city*).

The great sandstone mass on which Nottingham Castle is built rises a sheer 150 feet above river level; at its base, virtually beneath the Castle, lies an inn which has a better claim than most to be the oldest in England: its wall bears the date 1189 A.D. Why the name? 'Trip' has an older meaning: 'Halt'. And here it is said the Knights-Templar rallying to Richard I's Holy Crusades used to meet en route to the port.

It was doubtless smaller, then; but now, as then, it is largely a congeries of small rooms quite literally carved out of the friable sandstone of Castle Rock. You can see this for itself. Here and there in ceilings or walls grow plants whose roots may be traced to natural clefts fifty feet and more away; in the cavern-like cellars an orifice may be seen that connects, through a natural 'fault' in the rock, with the Castle, and was probably used by the stewards ordering ale from what was then the Castle's brew-house; at every turn there are 'hidey-holes', now objects of curiosity, but once vital factors in the lives of hunted men. Mortimer's Hole is one such: as Queen Isabella's lover he was sought by Edward III, and all her pleas could not save him from Tyburn six hundred years ago. In these various rock chambers there are relics of many kinds: skulls, an 'Armada Chest', rusted keys, and their massive padlocks which once sealed the stocks that stood in front of the inn.

Admittedly there is 'the smell of earth' here; but this is acceptable in view of the site, the history and the character of the building. And once in every generation, the smell of soot, when one extraordinary chimney is swept—involving the removal of a wall—and no less than eight tons of soot taken from it! You would think it was the Castle overhead that was having its many ancient chimneys swept.

THE GEORGE, Dorchester, Oxfordshire (*On A243, nine miles south of Oxford*).

The antique carriage standing outside offers a hint of the history of this inn; but in fact the inn was already ancient when coachbuilder and wheelwright picked up their tools. Eight centuries ago an Augustinian Priory was established here, and for much of the time the inn has been closely associated with it. When you stand looking up the high-raftered dining-hall you are in fact in the original monks' brew-house; you are unlikely to find a nobler example of interior half-timbering in such a building the length and breadth of the country.

But it was more than a monks' brewery. It was established five, perhaps six centuries ago as a hospice for visitors to the abbey, the ancient church of which is to be seen behind the gateway and stone wall immediately opposite. And that it was designed to accommodate travellers is clearly to be seen when you pass under the long square archway and enter the great cobbled yard behind. Glance up to your left and you will see that most rare survival of medieval times: the galleried 'Travellers' Lodgings', reached by an outside staircase. There is, too, the evidence of a former Minstrels' Gallery, a reminder that a licence for singing and dancing is no new thing.

The contrast between white façade, with clean-cut windows and lofty roof, and the oak timbering of the courtyard, the long gallery with doors opening off into dark rooms, once used by travellers, is marked. History is spread wide, here: beneath one roof you encounter the medieval, the monastic associations, the ghosts of the coaching era, when the Duchess of Marlborough, driving between London and Blenheim Palace, used to break her tedious journeys here, and the near-contemporary scene, with traffic swirling through a village that was formerly the capital of the Kingdom of Mercia.

THE TROUT, Godstow, Oxfordshire (*Off A34, three miles north of Oxford*).

Just one hundred years ago, Lewis Carroll took three children on a river picnic. 'We rowed up to Godstow, and had tea beside a haystack', he told a colleague of his at Christchurch College, Oxford, afterwards; 'I told them the fairy tale of Alice's adventures in Wonderland'.

Had his young guests been adults, he might have taken them into the *Trout Inn*, hard by. There has been a building on that foundation for at least seven centuries, and for more than half that time the building has been a hostelry. You can approach it by road, across the fields, or by the river, mooring at its waterside threshold. Almost certainly you will find yourself in the company of whole coveys of male and female undergraduates, for this inn has been a meeting-place for them for generations. Two storeys in height, of grey stone blocks, with generous leaded windows, two fine chimneys and a roof of Stonesfield slates, it stands four-square above the Thames, facing a tree-shaded garden and with the water of the famous lasher pouring swiftly down into the main stream almost below the picturesque signboard.

When you have inspected the Tudor hearth at one end of the main room, and the medieval hearth at the other, and looked up at the great oak beams, so finely preserved over the centuries, you may be inclined to think its interior, with its sporting prints by 'Phiz' and its engravings of Oxford by Turner, more impressive even than the exterior. But go outside again: consider the gently flowing stream, the shining weir, the strutting peacocks; and the ruins of the ancient nunnery near by, last home of Henry II's mistress, Rosamunde, one of the most tragic Royal Mistresses in all history. This is the seductive setting of this very ancient inn.

WHITCHURCH, Oxfordshire (*On B471, one mile north of Pangbourne*).

Here is, literally, a 'backwater' of a village, for slender arms of the Thames penetrate it in all directions. You approach it cautiously, by way of a toll-bridge, and the sixpence you pay there is a modest sum indeed for what awaits you. Immediately you have crossed the bridge you find yourself in what, for a lover of boats, water and the easeful life, of quietude and simplicity, must be near-paradise. The small waterways thread their way unobtrusively, crossed by a footbridge here, another there, intersecting gardens gay with colour, carrying dinghies and motor-launches that are moored beneath pergolas of roses, wattle fences or garage eaves. Small paths are interwoven with the waterways. One will lead you across the well-kept churchyard to a flower-filled garden out of which there rises, unexpectedly until you have become adjusted to the scene, the superstructure of a handsome cabin-cruiser; beneath the arch linking two halves of another garden peer the bows of a speed-boat, with cockle-shell dinghy nestling alongside, both nosing into the sunshine in the hope of action.

Every detail here has a nautical flavour. The local inn is named the Ferryboat. It has windows in its walls; but it has also a number of meticulously polished brass port-holes. You will not encounter many people wandering about the village; why? Because to almost all of them water takes precedence over land and so they are either already afloat or preparing to take to the water within the hour. Nevertheless, you may catch the hum of a motor-mower in the churchyard or on some private lawn running down to the water's edge. Or—is it a motor-boat, already edging her way down some small private waterway to the main stream? Perhaps. Come again a century, two centuries, hence: nothing is likely to have fundamentally changed.

MAINSTONE, Shropshire (*Just west of A488, four miles north of Clun*).

There is only one road into this minute hamlet: an extremely narrow and tortuous lane between high hedges. You must leave by the same way—unless you are prepared to take Shanks's Mare and clamber steeply out over springy turf. Indeed, really you should do this; for then you would be identifying yourself with Mainstone's chief, perhaps only, claim to distinction: the fact that it lies athwart King's Offa's Dyke.

Nearly twelve centuries ago this Mercian king had an earth rampart and ditch constructed over the fifty leagues between Chepstow in the south and Prestatyn in the north. It remains one of the most impressive but least regarded of all man's 'signatures' on the face of Britain. You may stand in the little cemetery surrounding the modest church and see this great rampart sweeping down like a giant whiplash off the southern hillside, to flatten out among the graves and then swing northwards up the opposing slope, to vanish over the horizon. For much of its way the Dyke forms the frontier between Wales and England; in that churchyard you may stand with a foot in each country, the graves making common purpose about your feet.

Look southwards: the Dyke is climbing to its highest point, on Llanvair, in what was once the great Forest of Clun. That is five miles—or is it five thousand miles? —from Mainstone, which now lies in this sleepy hollow of turf having forgotten the strife between Welshman and Mercian that raged here twelve hundred years ago. In a spot so calm, so sequestered, so silent, as this it is difficult indeed to believe that passions here could ever have run high, with pillage and retaliation, cattle- and wife-stealing and the frontier disputes so familiar to us today.

THE GEORGE & PILGRIMS INN, Glastonbury, Somerset (*On A39, fifteen miles east of Bridgwater*).

But for its signboard you might be excused for assuming that this magnificent building was the entrance to an Oxford college transported bodily to this ancient religious centre, the Mecca of the West, sometimes called 'the holiest place on earth'. Three storeys high, with a battlemented top, it has a superb bay window carried up the full height, with mullions and trefoil mouldings such as you would expect to see only in some great church. Indeed, there is an ecclesiastical touch to the façade, echoed within. Nor is this really surprising: for it was built almost exactly five centuries ago by Abbot John de Selwood to house worthily the better-class visitors to his abbey. It was, indeed, an outstanding example of a Church House.

The sign confirms its purpose. Originally named after St George, it soon took on the additional word that explains its use. Today it is loosely known as 'The George'; but those who sojourn beneath its roof, within its glorious panelled walls, have almost certainly come as twentieth-century pilgrims to steep themselves in the ancient traditions of this most holy place. They have come to see the ruins of the great abbey which, it is said, Henry VIII watched burning from one of these windows; to climb the hill to the spot where Joseph of Arimathea is said to have planted his staff, which became a thorn tree that flourished for fourteen centuries and blossomed annually on Christmas Day; to visit the tomb where he is said to have been buried, and the well where he is said to have hidden the Holy Grail exactly nineteen hundred years ago. Here, too, you are in King Arthur's legendary Isle of Avalon. Is it any wonder that this remains a place of pilgrimage? Times have changed, but the façade of the inn has not: through its fine portal five centuries of pilgrims have passed.

YE OLDE KINGS ARMS, Litton, Somerset (*On B3114, seven miles north of Shepton Mallet*).

If you are travelling fast, you may miss this attractive inn altogether, for it lies below the level of the road, largely screened by the downward slope of its spacious lawns and flower-filled garden. Whether or not it is one of the many inns where King Charles II is believed to have taken refuge, it is scheduled as a building of historic interest. Its brilliant white façade, with black-painted woodwork below a pantiled roof, with a fine cypress growing to roof height at its near end and an unexpected castellated entrance porch jutting boldly outwards, it invites inspection.

The immediate impression within is of age. The great stone slabs of the floor are smooth with the patina of age and a myriad restless feet; the thick walls and small windows imply snugness, security; the great open fireplaces speak of warmth and good fellowship dating from the days when the masons engaged on building the church near by forgathered here five centuries ago. There are features of especial interest in the bar. One is an enormous oak settle near the door, so huge that it can never have been brought through the door. It must either have been constructed inside the house, or introduced in sections and assembled here. Near by is a massive oak table with highly polished top marked out for what seems to have been an early form of the popular game of Shove-halfpenny. You will find it in a corner known still as the 'Tippet Room'—tippet being an old form of gambling which has doubtless been superseded in this more sophisticated age of Bingo and other modern crazes.

Glance back as you leave: you may not have noticed the unusual sign on the front of the inn: fashioned like a massive volume, vertical on a panel and opened wide to display the name of the inn, shown nearer the road as the more traditional inn-sign.

THE ROYAL OAK, Winsford, Somerset (*Off A396, twelve miles north of Bampton*).

This lovely old thatched inn is the centre-piece of one of our most beautiful villages, lying in a hollow in the heart of Exmoor. The Exe, not far from its source, flows past it; beneath a pack-horse bridge overlooked by the inn flows a tributary, the Winn, on its babbling way to the ford which gave the village its name. The music of running water is ever present, blended with that of the breeze in the foliage of a fine Scotch fir that rises from a circlet of stones by the end gable of the inn.

The close-set thatch slopes down over the gables, over the gabled porches that shelter the doorways, and curve protectively about the upper walls. Enter, and you find unexpectedly spacious rooms opening one from the other. Upstairs, a long corridor gives access to a succession of snug bedrooms. Its floor is uneven, there is a twist in the walls, dark oak beams cut through angles of white plasterwork from the roof immediately above you. Look out from any window, and you find the thatch so close that it fits like a massive collar. If you stay here in winter, this thatch will insulate you from the cold; and in summer, its generous depth will insulate you equally from the sun that pours down on this sequestered, sheltered spot. Upstairs or downstairs, this is a hostelry of character and charm; you will not be surprised to learn that it was the 'model' on which the *Britannia Inn* was designed for the British Exhibition held some years ago in New York.

It is beautifully sited, too. It faces a triangle of turf shaded by tall trees, where a permanent skittle-alley has been laid out. Beyond this, on a rise to the west, stands the Church of St Mary Magdalene, with its imposing tower. It offers a notable view of this hamlet of cob-walled cottages clustered about its own inn.

ALLERFORD, Somerset (*Just off A39, two miles east of Porlock*).

The focal point of this hamlet, nestling at the foot of the Allerford Woods, that clothe the steep slopes rising to Selworthy Beacon, is the medieval pack-horse bridge. Spanning the Aller stream just before it spills into Porlock Bay, it is one of the finest in the country. Between the stone parapets, low built to avoid dislodging the ponies' packs, the track is of pebbles set edgewise in cement to afford a sure grip for hooves and feet alike over the steep hump. Beyond, the track leads gently, then more steeply, upwards, soon to be lost in the Woods which, like the bridge and much of the village itself, are National Trust Property.

Before you follow it, take a look at the house alongside you. It is built of the warm red sandstone of the region. A porch almost on the bridge is dominated by an ancient and enormous walnut tree that has grown steeply away from the wall as though in lifelong search of sunlight and air. Its huge boughs have had to be buttressed on massive poles to prevent their crashing down into the ford alongside the bridge. No one in the village recalls when those buttresses were inserted.

Glance, too, at the chimney of this house. It is built in a style characteristic of this part of the West Country: cylindrical instead of square and clinging to the face of the wall though rising well above it, and of the same attractive ruddy stone. But unlike the majority of such chimneys—the well-known one at Porlock, for instance —it has not been cream washed; instead, it has been left in its natural state, as though it had grown, with the passing of the centuries, like some exotic climbing plant over the sheer sandstone wall which it so beautifully adorns. Above the pantiled roof it is finely silhouetted against the close-set foliage of the trees.

DUNSTER, Somerset (*Off A39, three miles east of Minehead*).

There can be few villages in all England owning so spacious a main street as that which graces Dunster. Indeed, viewed from either its lower or its upper end, it is more of a square, or 'place', than a street. Such traffic as uses it seems rather to linger than pass through—and who shall blame it? Half a mile to the north, traffic bound to or from the West Country may roar past on A 39; fortunately, most of it is in too much of a hurry to turn aside and cover the few hundred yards that lead to the upper end of the village. You enter it between the four-centuries-old, many-pillared Yarn Market on your right and the glorious façade of *The Luttrell Arms,* built five centuries ago as a town house for an abbot, on your left. You catch your first breath-taking view of the great pile of fourteenth-century Dunster Castle rising triumphant from its plinth of close-set trees beyond the cluster of lowlier buildings that make up the village. A road winds past them, sweeping up along the old track that divides Exmoor and the Brendon Hills, bound for Bampton and its Pony Fair.

You may be tempted not to leave this street, with its buildings of stone, brick, timber, tile and thatch, some ancient, some no older than Queen Anne. Resist the temptation, explore the narrow lanes branching off to the west. Here is a fine building with thrusting upper storeys, once a nunnery; here the Castle Mill, with its unusual double wheel; here a pack-horse bridge spanning the stream that once turned it. On every hand, indeed, a cream-washed cottage, creeper bedecked, tucked away behind a street that has long forgotten those busy years when cloth merchants congregated by day at the Yarn Market and by night among the medieval timbers of *The Luttrell Arms.*

BUTT & OYSTER, Pin Mill, Suffolk (*Off A138, six miles south-east of Ipswich*).

You smell sea water long before you come to the end of the narrow lane that terminates abruptly at the water's edge—the Orwell estuary. This is a place that has known ships down the centuries: ships, ship-building, sailors, fishermen, long-shoremen. Nor, you will rightly guess, has it changed overmuch down those centuries. You look on Thames and coastal barges, small yachts, a tug or two, a coastwise tramp or two with anchors down; on builders' yards, warehouses, ship-chandlers' premises. And, in the heart of them all, the inn which has been a meeting-place for four hundred years or so. Seafaring men frequent it, whether barge crews or deep-water yacht crews (though the landlubber is welcome too).

The sign portrays a barrel and some oysters. In fact, however, the 'Butt' is a local word for the flounder—as any Dutchman will confirm. Oysters are no longer to be taken here, for river pollution has spelt their end; but the flounder survives in shoals for the taking. The inn bearing this confusing if picturesque sign has been in its day, curiously enough, a Naval Court House; but all is freedom here today. You sit beneath massive beams, the ceiling joists supported by oaken 'knees' obviously once supporting a ship's deck. Old oak panelling surrounds you. Its wide windows hang out over the water. From them, generations of sailors and yachtsmen and sea-lovers generally have gazed at the wide expanse of estuary and southwards toward Harwich, four miles away. From here the yachts set out on their annual Harwich-Hook of Holland race. The inn has been the official and unofficial head-quarters of many yacht clubs large and small, a gathering-ground for enthusiasts in sail. At Pin Mill the great oak pegs for uniting ships' timbers were traditionally turned: hence the name of the tiny waterside village.

YE OLD BELL & STEELYARD, Woodbridge, Suffolk (*On B1438*).

For the collector of the unusual, this inn is a 'must'. Only one other in the whole country possesses its outstanding feature, and that one is in every way inferior to it. This feature—the first to catch your eye as you ascend or descend the steep road that passes beneath it—dominates the scene, almost overpowers it by its sheer weight, as though it would crush anything less than the massive oak timbers of the inn's façade that are dwarfed by its presence. All but one, that is: the enormous rough-hewn oak bole that takes the main weight of the gantry overhead, with its gabled cover and projecting steelyard, that looms over your head like some monstrous gibbet surviving from an older age.

What is its purpose, in fact? It was designed to enforce conformity with an edict that wagonloads should not exceed three tons. Every wagonload of barley or rye passing through the town had to halt, have its team unhitched, and then be lifted bodily off the ground by this steelyard. Penalties were severe. Within the oak and plaster walls of the inn, farmers, maltsters and carriers drowned their frustration, or celebrated their success, quaffing the inn's good ale. The inn, much of it of unmistakable fifteenth-century workmanship, was at once a menace and a solace. Today the menace has departed, but the solace remains. As you drink your beer or other tipple beneath its roof you may cast a glance at an enormous silvered iron block that now rests in the fireplace. It weighs perhaps a hundredweight. In its day it hung on that impressive steelyard, level with the eaves: it was the balancing-weight that told Authority in this small Suffolk market town whether it was being obeyed or not; an early weighing-device against which there was no appeal.

KERSEY, Suffolk (*Just west of B1070, two miles from Hadleigh*).

The focal point of this 'lost' village is the tree-shaded watersplash into which its single street dips and from which it emerges to climb to the church on the hill and the great world beyond. Once this was a famous and prosperous 'wool town', as the glorious flush-flint and stone Church of St Mary indicates. But it has fallen asleep; surely no village, even in Suffolk, its heyday being past, sleeps more soundly?

In the other direction the street climbs from the watersplash to the village pump; it is now chained, but it was in regular use not many years ago. The *White Horse Inn* on the corner reminds the passer-by that pump water is not the only form of refreshment. A few yards down the hill stands a pair of half-timbered houses on a plinth of most unusual brickwork, all the more attractive for their lack of sophistication, for they are wholly unrestored and are thus reminders of the inexorable passage of time. Below them, a second inn, *The Bell*: does a community so small, you wonder, really require a pump, a watersplash and two taverns into the bargain?

But inevitably, you are back at the watersplash, having passed a cottage or two, post-office and general store. That watersplash, dark water glinting beneath overhanging willows, draws you like a magnet. You cross by the footbridge. There is a glimpse of a fine Tudor manor-house set back among the trees beyond the willows. A writer of breathlessly exciting adventure yarns has made it his home: perhaps subconsciously seeking here the tranquillity he so deliberately excludes from his books. Kersey has this to offer him; nor is it ever likely to change, down the generations, even down the centuries ahead.

THE CROWN, Chiddingfold, Surrey (*On A283, twelve miles south of Guildford*).

Originally a Rest House for Cistercian monks on pilgrimage from Winchester to Canterbury, this ancient and splendid hostelry dates from the end of the thirteenth-century. A Deed in the hall there shows that it was let to a brewer in Chaucer's day, for the annual payment of—four shillings! In the mid-sixteenth-century Edward VI and his Court slept here, while his retinue of four thousand men camped on the spacious green overlooked by its windows. The old smithy opposite may well have supplied shoes to replace those cast along the road by the knights' horses.

Few inns are more dominating, make a greater impact, than this. You see a magnificent spread of fine oak timbering, a steeply-pitched roof, finely proportioned lattice windows, noble chimneys; you are aware of a sense of solidity, stability, comfort, and tradition. Moreover, it is beautifully and fittingly sited, in the heart of one of England's most beautiful villages, with a spacious railed pond, a twelfth-century church, and cottages and a shop or two to complete the picture, all framed in a glorious array of trees.

Within, the lounge bar is in what was the Great Hall of the original building, extending through two storeys to the high roof. Many of the huge timbers are now 'lost' in the ceilings and upper plasterwork, but you can still discover them if you are persistent. A noble stone fireplace bears the date 1584 and the oddly spelt name 'Jhon Knight' inscribed on the lintel. And just inside the doorway is an object interesting in itself, if out of keeping with the main fabric: an eighteenth-century sedan-chair. Glance again, and you will find that a telephone has been installed inside it. You make your call on the brocaded seat where, two centuries ago, some silk-clad beauty sat and was carried by her bearers to some romantic rendezvous!

YE OLD BELL, Oxted, Surrey (*On A25, seven miles east of Redhill*).

Opinions vary as to the true age of this fine old half-timbered inn; some say it was built in the thirteenth-century, others put it at a century or two later. Anyway, it stands close enough to the ancient Pilgrims Way to have been a regular halting-place for generations of pilgrims, monks and laymen alike, bound to and from Canterbury. It is well sited to catch the eye: at the top of a steep, narrow lane where it meets the west-east road running out of Surrey into Kent. The stone plinth that supports it is breast-high on the level road, and twice that height as the lane drops steeply away to a cottage garden or two and the tree-grown hills in the background.

From the plinth rises a white-painted brick wall intersected by massive black oak pillars braced by diagonals, among which small lead-paned windows strive to catch the light. The wall supports no fewer than forty oak joists, the protruding ends of which carry a massive beam that bears the entire weight of the overhanging upper storey, with its curved and interlacing beams, tiny windows and steeply-pitched roof. Forming a pleasing contrast with the half-timbering is the rear end of the house, beyond the steps that climb the plinth, which is faced with hanging pantiles.

On the corner, where lane and road intersect, high overhead, a beautiful ornate wrought-iron bracket carries, not a swinging sign but a curiously modelled bell that swings leisurely in the air that stirs about the upper timbers beneath the eaves. The bell, the inn's symbol, is oddly repeated elsewhere, in the form of a half-bell sunk in the plasterwork of a small gable. It is worth your while to linger here, at the tempo of those old pilgrims, to listen for the echo of the centuries when this old inn itself was young and feeling its way into the life of the time.

THE WHITE HART, Witley, Surrey (*On A283, eight miles south of Guildford*).

Six centuries ago, King Richard II built himself a hunting-lodge here. It was a barn-like structure of heavy oak timbers with a central hearth on a stone floor, from which the smoke escaped through a hole in the roof. The smoke preserved the timbers sufficiently for the barn to be extended, later, sideways and upwards; you can inspect them today. The sense of antiquity is greater, here, within than without. Though the central open hearth has been replaced by a fireplace in the wall, the flue is so large that for centuries hams were suspended in it from the 'curing-room' immediately above for smoking in season. There are deep ingle-nooks, one of them named after the author, George Eliot, who wrote much of *Daniel Deronda* beneath this roof. Behind the ingle-nooks is a second bar, formerly the stables of the royal hunters, as its beams clearly reveal. And overhead, on the superimposed upper floor a century or two less ancient than the ground floor, a labyrinth of bedrooms and corridors winds hither and yon, intersected by massive beams, warmed from the great hearth below.

In the cobbled courtyard beneath the windows the famous Witley Friday Market, instituted seven centuries ago, used to be held; five centuries later, the inn received its first licence. It is justifiably proud of its sign: a finely painted hart set against a colourful background on a great square panel framed by the pantiles beneath the diamond-paned dormer window in the roof. Standing beneath it, you look across the cobbles at a beautiful half-timbered cottage, 'Steps Cottage', taking its name from a flight of steps that lead you into the adjacent Church of All Saints. Among its Norman masonry, if you look carefully, you will descry a rare example of a true Saxon window, facing across the lane, down the steps, to the neighbouring inn.

ABINGER HAMMER, Surrey (*On A25, six miles east of Guildford*).

The village does not, as you might suppose, take its name from the 'Jack' who stands high above the dog's-leg corner on the road, mounted beneath the black and gold clock of the Clock House and striking every hour with his hammer on the bell. He is audibly illustrating the verse behind him: 'For You at Home I Part the Day, Work and Play Twixt Sleep and Meals'. He looks out over the village green, memorial to the Abinger men who died in World War I; it is fringed on one side by a charming row of tile-hung cottages whose windows make an excellent grandstand for the cricket played there.

No, the 'hammer' in the name is an echo of the past, when, strange as it must seem today, this was a thriving industrial centre. Here the good iron ore of the district was smelted and forged. There was ample fuel in the surrounding forests; and ample power for the big trip-hammers was supplied by the waters of the Tillingbourn, a stream which still flows placidly past the green, its generous waters no longer harnessed. Above the village, beside the road, you may still see the giant pounds, excavated to contain a sufficient head of water for the rapacious hammers. Today they have been converted to the growing of watercress. Follow the stream down towards the village and you come upon the great stones of the dam and sluices; and the massive mountings of those hammers which once thudded unceasingly in this quiet place. Gardeners have only to dig a foot or so down through the topsoil to come upon the grey-black powder of smelting. And it was only recently that men excavating in a builder's yard on the site of the smelting works, once so busy, dug up a massive cannon-ball—a reminder that even in those relatively placid days, the end-product of a quiet village possessed lethal qualities.

SHEPHERD & DOG, Fulking, Sussex (*Off A23, four miles north-west of Brighton*).

This truly rural inn is perched on a corner at the foot of a short, steep lane rising to the little hamlet of Fulking. If you approach the hill too fast you may well miss it; and this would indeed be to miss a little gem.

It is set into the lower slopes of the Downs, below Devil's Dyke, and evidently on the line of an ancient sheep-droving route between downland pastures and market and fair. It has a long tradition of never-failing water—a vital consideration on these dry chalklands.

Beside the inn, a spring flows strongly out of a bank, to run to waste along the lane. Inscribed on the well-house above it are the pious words that hold a meaning for men and sheep dependent on this water: 'He Sendeth Springs into the Valleys Which Run among the Hills. Oh that Men would Praise the Lord for His Goodness!'

Though so small, the inn has three signboards. One portrays a Sussex shepherd in full-length smock seated at the open inn door with a quart jug of ale on his knee and his dog at his feet. Another shows him wearing his hard, tall, flat-crowned hat and holding his locally-made crook as he stands silhouetted against the galleon clouds of a windswept sky, his sheep, like small cloudlets, on the green turf behind him. The third sign is a small cut-out of a smocked shepherd with crook and dog at heel striding urgently across the Downs. The inn itself is painted a pleasing shrimp-pink. Low slung, it is partly hidden by a wall of flint ten feet high at the foot of the hill, tapering to a few inches at the entrance: a measure of the steepness of the hill, at the foot of which generations of shepherds have lingered to water their flocks, and to drink a welcome glass of ale while they do so.

THE STAR, Alfriston, Sussex (*On B2108, five miles west of Eastbourne*).

Few ancient inns have fulfilled the same function throughout their existence; this one is an exception. Built and owned by the Abbot of neighbouring Battle Abbey, it was designed as a hostel for pilgrims journeying to the shrine of St Richard, at Chichester. The building dates from the middle of the fifteenth-century, and has hardly changed in five hundred years. Its massive oak timbers, its solid yet delicate oriel windows jutting forth from the roof of huge slabs of Horsham stone, many of them weighing little short of a hundredweight, the great moulded oak beam, massive as a ship's keel that carries the projecting upper floor: these are still as those pilgrims knew them. Indeed, so hard is the oak that the figures carved in it by the medieval craftsmen are still clearly to be seen: a mitred bishop, two snakes with intertwined tails, St Michael fighting the Basilisk (NOT St George and the Dragon, as many think), the lion and monkey, and the oddly appealing little terrier; all are still there.

Before entering, stop and look at the weird totem-like figure on the corner beneath that jutting upper storey, the lion-jawed head on a stump of a body. It was once the figurehead of a ship wrecked a mere three centuries ago on the coast a few miles away—almost modern in comparison with the antiquity of the inn itself. Now enter. Beams everywhere, stout as ship's masts, roughly squared; a glorious Tudor fireplace with roasting-jack still in position; a great staircase rising from the brick floor. This is how it always was; the interior, too, is little changed since the first pilgrims entered it. An ecclesiastical foundation, named piously after the 'Star of Bethlehem'; its atmosphere clings to it yet, like a ghostly aura.

THE SWAN, Fittleworth, Sussex (*Off A283, three miles east of Petworth*).

After crossing a pair of hump-backed bridges you pass beneath a wooden gantry from which there hangs the signboard of this inn. Take a good look at it, for it is one of the beautiful inn signs painted by Ralph Ellis, whose work is to be found in so many corners of the county. Above the signboard, on a lovely wrought-iron framework, are two shields, bearing the arms of the Duke of Norfolk and Lord Leconfield.

Do not enter the inn at once. Rather, walk on a hundred yards up the sloping village street and then turn about. You see a white stone façade topped by a tile-hung upper storey beneath a low-pitched roof. This in itself is an object of beauty, for it undulates gently the full length of the building, as though the weight of the heavy Horsham slates over the years had proved more than the rafters could comfortably sustain. Two ornate lamps hang from wrought-iron brackets above the doors; and two old mangers are attached to the lower wall, each filled with growing plants. You pass between these, to enter an inn that has been a favourite haunt of anglers and of artists for generations past.

Anglers and artists: the first because there has always been good fishing in the streams that flow beneath the bridges immediately behind the inn and through the spacious water-meadows; and it is easy to see why artists have always found this place an inspiration for their work. Evidence of this may be found in the small lounge: some forty of the panels surrounding this room have been painted by nineteenth-century artists who have relaxed here, and when, reluctantly, they have had to take their departure, have been happy to leave behind them these highly individual mementoes of their appreciation.

AMBERLEY, Sussex (*Off B2139, five miles north of Arundel*).

Here is a village fortunate enough to lie just off a busy road. It is poised on a low terrace, overlooking the Arun as it twists its way south to the coast, sheltered by the South Downs from northerly winds, a sun trap half the year round. Its single street leads to the shell of a fourteenth-century castle, once the property of the bishops of Chichester ten miles to the west. It stands almost in the churchyard of the even older Church of St Michael, one of the most beautiful in all Sussex, whose Norman chancel-arch with its zigzag moulding is worth a long journey to see.

But somehow it is not so much the castle or the church that remains in the memory after one has left it; rather, it is the atmosphere of the village as a whole. For here is serenity embodied. Moreover, it is an entity composed of most perfectly matched parts. Almost every building in it is of warm grey-brown stone; the thatch undulates over dormer windows and gables like thick moleskin; small upper windows peep beneath bushy eyebrows; woodwork is painted yellow, blue, green; the chimneys are tall and characterful, built to take smoke high over the thatched roofs.

And the gardens! Where cottages front immediately on to the road there are two-foot-wide channels of stone raised from road level, filled with flowers, to form a gay, lively plinth. Here and there a border of flowers runs atop a ten-foot wall, and inspection reveals that it is the edge of a garden level with upper-floor windows. Trees overhang the further end of the street, so that you pass from the sun-drenched centre of the village into a cool oasis of shade as you approach the castle and church and the glint of silver water in the water-meadows beyond. A seat in the churchyard records that a year or two ago this was the best-kept village in Sussex.

LINDFIELD, Sussex (*On B2028, two miles north of Hayward's Heath*).

Your approach is across a spacious common where cricket matches are regularly played. Thence the road curves like a whiplash round the village pond, framed by a curving low brick wall and alive with cruising swans. Cottage gardens slope to the water, with banks of flowers, rose-clad pergolas and lawns overhung by weeping-willows. From the pond's edge the road climbs gently between two rows of limes growing in wide grass verges—Lindfield means 'the place of the lime trees'—to the Church of All Saints, with its Sussex-style broach spire.

Secluded behind high hedges and mellow brick walls lie dwelling-houses of many architectural styles and periods, from Elizabethan by way of Queen Anne to near-modern. Strangely, though, these variegated buildings blend with one another, as though the age and acquired serenity of this lovely place had exerted a beneficent influence upon all alike, gathering them together into one family unit.

You may well think that the most beautiful and memorable of these buildings is the finely preserved twin house known as 'The Well House' and 'Barnlands'. Here are magnificent oak timbers framing patterns of brickwork; over all, a splendid roof of massive Horsham stone slabs, many of which must weigh a hundredweight and more apiece: proof of the sturdiness of the Sussex oak roof timbers and the care and skill of the men who set them in place all those centuries ago.

More famous, perhaps, is the Elizabethan Old Place, tucked away behind the church. Formerly the home of the Chaloners, it still suggests the richly endowed life of a community that has changed so little since the days of the First Elizabeth.

LONG COMPTON, Warwickshire (*On A34, four miles north of Chipping Norton*).

As its name suggests, this is a village stretched out along one street, to peter out at either end in open Cotswold country. You should enter it at the lower end of the rising street, marked by the Church of St Peter and St Paul on your left, standing among the yews planted in its spacious churchyard. The Norman doorways are worth your attention; more unusual, however, if less ancient, is the gatehouse beneath which you must pass to enter.

Two massive stone piers carry a small square half-timbered house, with one bold window fore and aft beneath a chimney and a roof of thatch. Known as 'The Priest's House', it was certainly occupied by a succession of vergers; and until but very recently, by the village cobbler. He could be seen at his last behind the disproportionately large window, to which he had mounted by a stairway inset in the stone wall. When he looked over his shoulder he could reflect on the symbols of death planted in the graveyard. Through his front window he looked towards the Stone Circle known as 'The Rollright Stones', the solitary 'King Stone' and the group of 'Whispering Knights', all so closely associated with this ancient village.

Long, long before even the Norman part of the church at his back was built, a king was leading his army to battle. A furlong or two away, he was halted by a witch. 'If Long Compton thou can see', she intoned, 'Then King of England shalt thou be!' But alas, the straggling village on the slope was hidden from his eyes by a veil of mist she conjured up; he and his men were turned to stone; she herself became an 'eldern tree'. You may see all this for yourself, from Long Compton.

RATTLEBONE INN, Sherston, Wiltshire (*On B4040, five miles west of Malmesbury*).

At the top of the hill, on the corner, just as the roads turns left and opens into Sherston's charming and spacious main street, stands this unpretentious village inn of whitewashed stone beneath its fine roof of local slabs. A few hanging baskets relieve its plain façade; but, colourful as are the flowers, they pale alongside the startlingly realistic inn-sign—the only one of the name in all England.

It depicts the magnificent, semi-legendary figure of John Rattlebone, a Saxon warrior who fought the Danish invaders at the great battle on the near-by Fosse. His right hand flourishes a massive two-edged broadsword, the business-end of which is stained deep in its victims' gore. Framed between sword and uplifted arm is a bearded face which registers an impressive blend of fury and barely-suppressed agony. Agony because he has just received a ghastly stomach wound. The left hand clutches a slab of local stone, pressing it hard against the stomach, 'to prevent his bowels gushing out'. A lesser man would have given up the fight; not so John Rattlebone! With the tile checking the flow of blood and guts, he fought on, the mound of dead Danes piled ever higher about his feet. The flowing orange cloak, the bright chain-mail, and the background of spears form a dramatic contrast to the smooth white wall behind the sign, that of a homely rural inn which has borne it for so many peaceful generations.

Just across the road at the corner, facing down the hill, stands the Church of the Holy Cross, half screened by a magnificent copper beech that overhangs the fine lych-gate. It is worth crossing the road to look at. Pause a moment in the porch. Does that stone effigy represent an old churchman holding a book? Or could it be a replica of old John Rattlebone clutching to his riven stomach that slab of local stone?

RATTLEBONE INN

RED LION, Avebury, Wiltshire (*On A361, six miles west of Marlborough*).

This attractive thatched and white-painted, partly half-timbered inn dates back more than four hundred years: old enough, you would doubtless say. But compared with its setting it is a mere babe-in-arms. For it stands at the very hub of the Avebury Stone Circle which, with the 'Avenue of Stone', constitutes one of the most famous megalithic monuments in the world. The Altar, which was at the centre of the Circle, lies right beneath the foundations of the inn; and the avenue of gigantic megaliths stretches southward from its very doorstep to Silbury Hill, the largest man-made earth mound in the world. Here, in an inn bearing one of the commonest of inn names, you stand at the heart of one of the world's oldest religious centres; you are linked with our own island's earliest civilisation.

Before you enter, though, spare a moment to examine the two old cider-presses now standing idle in the forecourt. One designed to be operated by a horse or mule, the other by mere manual labour. Their great stones bear visual evidence of generations of lusty use. Cider may have been brewed beneath this roof; the inn has always been self-sufficient; its water-supply was at its heart, as you may see.

When you enter its main room you will find, at floor level, the mouth of a well. Eighty feet deep, and narrower than most, the shaft plunges to a glint of clear water at its foot. It has been skilfully lit, so that you can trace the successive strata through which it was driven, three centuries and more ago. You may meanwhile be rubbing shoulders with archaeologists from all over the world, come here to study this megalithic monument, and the prehistoric culture that produced this incomparable Circle and Avenue, visible to you from any one of the windows of this inn.

148

CASTLE COMBE, Wiltshire (*Just off B4039, five miles west of Chippenham*).

The 'village in a nutshell'. It clings to the concave sides of a deep hollow, thus acquiring compactness. Three modest streets emerge from the all-embracing tree-clad hillsides, to converge in a small triangular 'square' with a beautiful, ancient market cross as its hub: stone steps, stone pillars at corners and centre, a steeply pitched slab roof topped by a delicate finial. Here, generations of vendors and customers have chaffered, breaking off now and then to wet their whistles either at *The Castle* or at *The White Hart*, facing one another across the square.

Every building here, whether church, manor-house behind it, diminutive cottage with banks of gay flowers forming a plinth beneath it, market cross or curving bridge at the foot of the street, is of stone from doorstep to roof and chimney. The cottages spill down the street almost helter-skelter, to be brought up short at the foot of the little bridge spanning a stream known to map-makers as By Brook but to Castle Combe folk as Weaver.

Perhaps this is the best vantage-point from which to survey the village. A slight twist in the mounting street affords you alternating glimpses of the cottages facing one another, and a half-glimpse of the market cross, the inevitable focal point. You ascend, leisurely savouring the beauty all about you: the banked flowers against the mellow stone, the lichen-softened slab roofs, the infinite variety of the gables and dormers, the glimpse of the church tower above the roofs. And the whole is set against a profusion of oak and ash, chestnut, sycamore and beech, clothing the encircling slopes. Is Castle Combe, perhaps, a shade self-conscious? Well, a beautiful woman, surely, is entitled to be aware of her gift of beauty, that can give pleasure to so many besides herself.

STEEPLE ASHTON, Wiltshire (*Just off A350, three miles east of Trowbridge*).

If you could roll back the centuries as you stand on the spacious green of this quiet village you would find a very different atmosphere. For this was once an important centre of the wool industry; its name is a corruption of the term 'staple', meaning this basic commodity brought to market; here, formerly, was a thriving wool merchants' gathering-ground.

Its charm today lies in its spaciousness; and in the variety of its architectural styles, so happily married. Stone, of course, predominates: it is to be seen in the fabric of those cottages fronting the green; in the medieval lock-up there; in the fabric of the fifteenth-century Church of St Mary the Virgin, whose noble tower, with its bright blue clock-face and gilded hands above the sundial on the South Porch, dominates the village and can be seen for miles around on this level plain. But there is brick, cob, and some notable half-timbering, too. You see it at its best in the row of old buildings facing the ancient market cross on the green and containing the post-office. The peculiar charm of this brickwork is to be found not only in its mellowness and rich colour but in the herringbone patterns which have been used with such effect.

From those small, shadowed windows you look straight across the wide road at the market cross, focal point of the village down the ages and meeting-place of the wool merchants. It is a stone column bearing four sundials, one for each compass-point, and each with a beautiful wrought-iron gnomon, variously mounted; the whole is topped by a stone sphere, which itself is surmounted by a golden crown. The sun glinting on this reminds us of the heyday of a village that has fallen asleep.

ELMLEY CASTLE, Worcestershire (*Off A44, four miles west of Evesham*).

This is a Vale of Evesham village: for anyone who knows the Vale, this is sufficient recommendation without further description! Its single street widens into a wedge-shaped square, on one corner of which stands the Queen Elizabeth Inn with its eye-catching signboard depicting the First Elizabeth on each side, though in different guise. Facing it is a fine building, once the refectory of the Monks' College. It epitomises the character of the village as a whole, for while its lower storey is of stone, its upper storey is half-timbered and its roof is of the sort of slab stone that predominates in the Cotswolds, which lie immediately to the south-east.

As in so many of these west Midlands villages, the architects have had their loyalties strained between the tradition of half-timbering, found at its finest along the Welsh Border, and that of the stone building that is the glory of the Cotswolds. In Elmley Castle the buildings stand elbow to elbow round the square and along the street, alternating between these two styles, each lovely in itself; they have grown so accustomed to one another's presence that they now blend most happily with one another: stone roof and thatch, half-timbering and stone façade, fine eighteenth-century rectangular windows set in brick neighbouring intimate dormer windows half hidden beneath the weight of their thatch.

From most of the windows you look out upon this secluded square, the well trimmed grass and shapely trees. In the square, beneath the swinging sign of the inn, the Morris Dancers annually perform; here, too, the hunt meets from time to time. And a hundred yards away, on the magnificent stretch of the village green, cricket matches are enthusiastically played and attended throughout the summer months.

154

BISHOP BURTON, Yorkshire (*On A1079, three miles west of Beverley*).

Most villages, if they are unfortunate enough to bestride a main road, tend to sprawl along its length and so lack cohesion. This village is an exception. Not much more than, perhaps, a hundred yards of road pass through it; but the cottages have been so placed as to lie within sight of and at the same time remote from it. Deliberately planned or not, the effect is most satisfying to the eye that dwells upon it.

The road by which you enter slopes gently downwards, to flatten out and curve left-handedly about the focal point of the village, a small, crescent-shaped lake fenced on the road side with white rails and posts, its clear, still waters occupied by a small flotilla of swans. It is backed by a coppice against which the War Memorial, beautifully sited and proportioned, stands out clearly but unemphatically. On either side of the road and the little lake, the cottages, whitewashed and individual, form an irregular fringe to the village. They look out across a generous stretch of green-sward to the road and the lake itself, and to a white-and-black-painted structure that was, until but the day before yesterday, the village pump water supply. An oak post with ornamental wrought-iron frame, and an oak seat, commemorate the fact that the village won an award as the best kept village in the East Riding.

The thirteenth-century tower of the Church of All Saints stands on a hillock behind the coppice, with a covey of cottages at its foot; and at the far end of the village you will find the *Altisidora Inn*, still known by its old name, 'Horse & Jockey', but commemorating a locally-bred winner, a century and a half ago, of the St Leger. It is attractively placed: half shaded by a fine stand of chestnuts, and overlooking a curve of bright water. Small wonder that passing traffic tends to slow down here.

STAITHES, Yorkshire (*Off A174, ten miles north-west of Whitby*).

The name means neither more nor less than 'landing-place'. If you entered it by the precipitous lane that leads down to it from the main road, you may be inclined to think that you would have done better to approach by boat. For the village lies, quite literally, in the bottom of a ravine. For aeons of time a swift beck has been chiselling its way ever deeper and more steeply through the strata of limestone that form these Yorkshire coastline headlands, to plunge into the sea. On its nearly vertical sides the cottages of this fishing village are precariously perched. Immediately to the north-west of the ravine, Boulby Cliff, the highest in England, rears its proud mass; its lesser brethren are ranged all along this dramatic coast.

The stream breaks out into a lobster claw-like bay, the two claws of which offer shelter to the village and the harbour from the storms that sweep the North Sea. Within that shelter lie the cobles of the fishermen who, like their forefathers for six centuries, still brave the tide-races and the lee shore to ply a trade that makes giants of them all. There are still lobsters and crabs and other fish to be caught; but it is a hazardous means of earning a speculative livelihood.

The buildings press upon you as you descend the steep hill. At its lower end it is so narrow that two bicycles can only just pass one another. Then it opens out into the harbour, with its medley of odours: tar, seaweed, decaying fish, preserving salt, lead paint and wet rope and lobster-pots. At your elbow is the appropriately named *Cod & Lobster* inn. Its sign portrays a lobster-pot containing a dejected fragment of cod; outside it, a giant lobster gazes both hungrily and warily upon the bait. You may see his fellows being landed from a coble at any hour of any day.

ACKNOWLEDGEMENTS

The author makes grateful acknowledgement to the following for permission to reproduce photographs in this book:

The British Travel Association for those facing pages 16, 20, 28, 36, 40, 42, 46, 48, 52, 54, 56, 62, 70, 74, 80, 82, 88, 100, 108, 116, 118, 124, 134, 140, 142, 144, 150 & 152; The Mustograph Agency for those facing pages 22, 76, 94, 96, 106, 122 & 126; Messrs. Charrington and Company for those facing pages 104 & 110; Messrs. Courage, Barclay and Simonds for that facing page 60; Messrs. Strong and Company for that facing page 66; Messrs. Trust House Hotels Limited for those facing pages 78 & 136; Messrs. Watney, Mann and Company for those facing pages 50 & 138; Messrs. West Country Breweries for that facing page 146; and Messrs. Whitbread and Company for that facing page 18.

The remainder of the photographs were specially taken by the author.

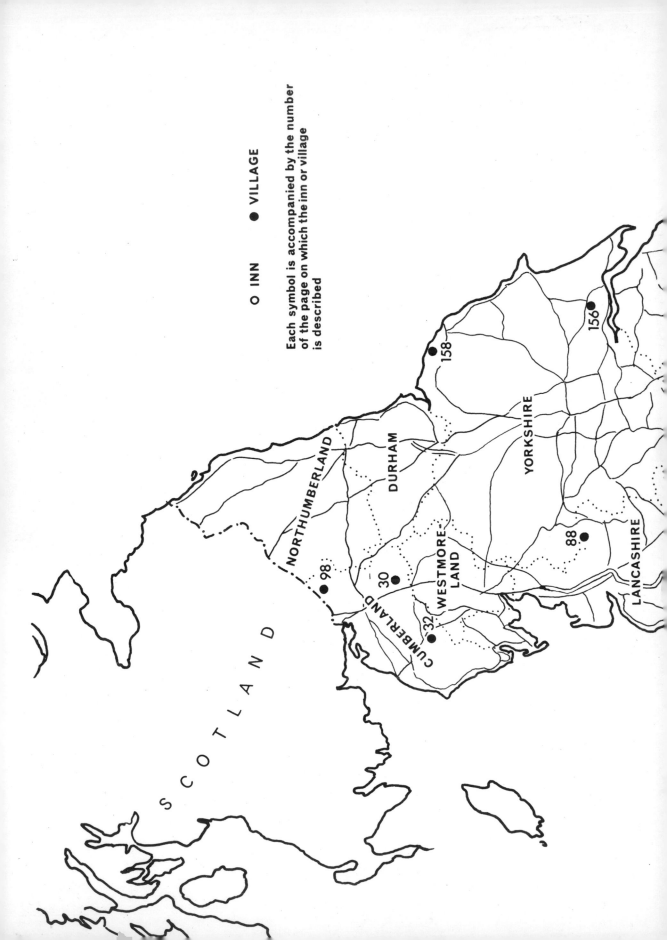

O INN   ● VILLAGE

Each symbol is accompanied by the number of the page on which the inn or village is described